BHAGAVAD-GITA

THE SONG OF GOD

FROM THE TOUCHSTONE

......This book is a notable addition to Gita literature.......It is a just and faithful interpretation.

—Rt. Hon. V.S. Srinivasa Sastri
in *The Hindu.*

......A distinguished literary work.

—*Time* (U.S.A.)

......The translators have......been able to make the translation delightful reading.

—*Hindustan Standard.*

For those who are willing to give the introduction and appendix the study they deserve, this version of the Gita is probably the best available. —*Times of India.*

We are now offered a readable, agreeable and heterodox version of the Gita, not a literal translation, nor all in verse.

—*Hindustan Review*

BHAGAVAD-GITA

The Song of God

TRANSLATED BY

Swami Prabhavananda

and

Christopher Isherwood

WITH AN INTRODUCTION BY

Aldous Huxley

Sri Ramakrishna Math

Mylapore, Chennai - 4

Published by
Adhyaksha
Sri Ramakrishna Math
Mylapore, chennai - 4

First Edition, February 1945
Twenty-fourth Print, September 2016
2M3C

ISBN 81-7120-160-1

Total number of copies printed till now: 65,600

Printed in India at
Sri Ramakrishna Math Printing Press
Mylapore, Chennai - 4

To
the memory of
SWAMI TURIYANANDA
who was regarded by his Master
SRI RAMAKRISHNA
as a perfect embodiment of that renunciation
which is taught in the
BHAGAVAD GITA

Introducing The Translators

Swami Prabhavananda is a disciple of Swami Brahmananda, first President of the Ramakrishna Mission and a direct disciple of Sri Ramakrishna. He has been doing Vedanta Work in the U.S. since 1923.

Christopher Isherwood is a well-known English author, listed amongst the notables in Webster's Biographical Dictionary, now in retirement in the Ramarkishna Ashrama, Hollywood.

Translators' Preface

Nowadays, it is becoming fashionable to translate the world's great books into some form of Basic English, or everday speech. The Gita does not easily lend itself to such treatment. The Sanskrit in which it is written differs radically from modern English. It is compressed and telegraphic. It abounds in exact philosophical and religious terms. Its frame of reference is a system of cosmology unfamiliar to western thought. And indeed, it would be hard to evolve any uniform English style, modern or ancient, in which the Gita could be satisfactorily rendered.

For, the Gita regarded simply as a piece of literature, is not a unity. It has several aspects, several distinct tones of voice. Let us consider each of them in turn.

First, the Gita may be regarded as part of an epic poem. It is all in verse. The first chapter is pure epic, continuing in the mood of the Mahabharata itself. The shouting of warriors, the neighing of horses and the outlandish names of chieftains are still sounding in our ears as the dialogue between Krishna and Arjuna begins. To translate this epic prologue as though it belonged to the philosophical discourse which follows would be to cut the Gita right out of its historical setting and deprive it of its vivid local colour.

Then, again, the Gita is an exposition of Vedanta philosophy, based upon a very definite picture of the universe. It is no use trying to disregard this fact, for fear of alienating the western reader. The translator who uses "reassuring" topical equivalents, and twists the meaning of the Sanskrit terms, may think he is building a bridge between two systems of thought, when actually he is reducing both of them to nonsense. We have tried to explain the cosmology of the Gita, as briefly as possible, in an appendix. Certain basic and much-used words, such as Brahman, Atman, Prakriti and the gunas, have been kept in Sanskrit, for the same reason. Precise English equivalents are lacking, and every book on philosophy or science must have a defined terminology. No one would write about physics and avoid using the word "electron," just because it does not occur in everyday speech.

The Gita is also prophetic. Like the Vision of Isaiah and the Psalms of David, it contains ecstatic mystical utterances about the nature and attributes of God. These are poetry, and demand poetic expression. The diction must try to correspond to the inspiration. Ordinary prose will render them flat and boring.

Finally, the Gita is a gospel. Its essential message is timeless. In words which belong to no one language, race or epoch, incarnate God speaks to man, His friend. Here, the translator must forget all about Vedanta philosophy and Sanskrit terms and about India and the West, Krishnas and Arjuna, past and future. He must aim at the utmost simplicity.

That is why we have translated the Gita in a variety of styles, partly prose partly verse. There is, of course, no justification for this experiment in the text itself. The transitions from on style to another are quite arbitrary. They can be judged from one standpoint only; have we made the book more readable?

Extremely literal translations of the Gita already exist. We have aimed rather, at an interpretation. Here is one of the greatest religious documents of the world; let us not approach it too pedantically, as an archaic text which must be jealously preserved by university professors. It has something to say, urgently, to every one of us. We have to extract that message from the terseness of the original Sanskrit, and here the great classical commentators can help us. In making this translation, three of them have been consulted throughout — Shankara, Sridhara Swami and Madhusudana Saraswati. Wishing to avoid bulky foot-notes, we have incorporated their explanations in our English version. Sri Aurobindo Ghose's masterly *Essays on the Gita* have also been helpful, Nevertheless, our work is not a paraphrase. Except in a very few difficult passages, it faithfully follows the original.

We have allowed ourselves one small liberty. The Gita is sprinkled with epithets. Krishna is called

"Govinda," "Slayer of Madhu," "Keshava," etc. Arjuna is addressed as "Consumer of the foe," "Son of Kunti," "Descendant of Bharata," "Son of Pritha," and much else. We have kept a few of these, in the opening chapters, to create "atmosphere." Later they are mostly omitted, unless they seem effective for purely literary reasons. Their repetition is apt to grow very tiresome.

In conclusion, we have to thank our friends, Margaret Adams Kiskadden and Aldous Huxley, for their help, frank criticism and warm encouragement. The final draft of our translation owes them much, perhaps its very existence.

Contents

Introduction

More than twenty-five centuries have passed since that which has been called the Perennial Philosophy was first committed to writing; and in the course of those centuries it has found expression, now partial, now complete, now in this form, now in that, again and again. In Vedanta and Hebrew prophecy, in the Tao Teh King and the Platonic dialogues, in the Gospel according to St. John and Mahayana theology, in Plotinus and the Areopagite, among the Persian Sufis and the Christian mystics of the

Middle Ages and the Renaissance—the Perennial Philosophy has spoken almost all the languages of Asia and Europe and has made use of the terminology and traditions of every one of the higher religions. But under all this confusion of tongues and myths, of local histories and particularist doctrines, there remains a Highest Common Factor, which is the Perennial Philosophy in what may be called its chemically pure state. This final purity can never, of course, be expressed by any verbal statement of the philosophy, however undogmatic that statement may be, however deliberately syncretistic.

The very fact that it is set down at a certain time by a certain writer, using this or that language, automatically imposes a certain sociological and personal bias on the doctrines so formulated. It is only in the act of contemplation, when words and even personality are transcended, that the pure state of the Perennial Philosophy can actually be known. The records left by those who have known it in this way make it abundantly clear that all of them, whether Hindu, Buddhist, Hebrew, Taoist, Christian or Mohammedan, were attempting to describe the same essentially indescribable Fact.

The original scriptures of most religion are poetical and unsystematic. Theology, which generally takes the form of a reasoned commentary on the parables aphorisms of the scriptures, tends to make its appearance at a later stage of religious history. The Bhagavad Gita occupies an intermediate position between scripture and theology; for it combines the poetical qualities of the first with the clear-cut methodicalness of the second. "The book may be described" writes Ananda K. Coomaraswamy in his admirable 'Hinduism and Buddhism' "as a compendium of the whole doctrine to be found in the earlier Vedas, Brahmanas and Upanishads, and being therefore the basis of all the later developments, it can be regarded as the focus of all Indian religion." But this 'focus of Indian religion' is also one of the—clearest and most comprehensive summaries of the Perennial Philosophy ever to have been made. Hence its enduring value, not only for Indians, but for all mankind.

At the core of the Perennial Philosophy we find four fundamental doctrines.

First: the phenomenal world of matter and of individualized

consciousness—the world of things and animals and men and even gods—is the manifestation of a Divine Ground within which all partial realities have their being, and apart from which they would be non-existent.

Second: human beings are capable not merely of knowing *about* the Divine Ground by inference; they can also realize its existence by a direct intuition, Superior to discursive reasoning. This immediate knowledge unites the knower with that which is known.

Third: man possesses a double nature, a phenomenal ego and an eternal Self, which is the inner man, the spirit, the spark of divinity within the soul. It is possible for a man, if he so desires, to identify himself with the Spirit and therefore with the Divine Ground, which is of the same or like nature with the Spirit.

Fourth: man's life on earth has only one end and purpose: to identify himself with his eternal Self and so to come unitive knowledge of the Divine Ground.

In Hinduism the first of these four doctrines is stated in the most categorical terms. The Divine Ground is Brahman, whose creative sustaining and transforming aspects are manifested in the Hindu trinity. A hierarchy of manifestations connects inanimate matter with man, gods, High Gods and the undifferentiated Godhead beyond.

In Mahayana Buddhism the Divine Ground is called Mind or the Pure Light of the Void, the place of the High Gods is taken by the Dhyani-Buddhas.

Similar conceptions are perfectly compatible with Christianity and have in fact been entertained, explicitly or implicitly, by many Catholic and Protestant mystics, when formulating a philosophy to fit facts observed by super-rational intuition. Thus, for Eckhart and Ruysbroeck, there is an Abyss of Godhead underlying the Trinity, just as Brahman underlying Brahma, Vishnu and Shiva. Suso has even left a diagrammatic picture of the relations subsisting between Godhead, triune God and creatures. In this very curious and interesting drawing a chain of manifestation connects the mysterious symbol of the Divine Ground with the three Persons of the Trinity, and the Trinity in turn is connected in a descending scale with angels and human beings. These last, as the drawing vividly shows, may make one of two choices. They can either lead the life of the outer man, the life of separative selfhood, in which case they are lost (for, in the words of the Theologia Germanica 'nothing burns in hell but the self'). Or else they can identify themselves with the inner man in which case it become possible for them, as Suso shows, to ascend again, through unitive knowledge, to the Trinity and even, beyond the Trinity, to ultimate Unity of the Divine Ground.

Within the Mohammedan tradition such a rationalization of the immediate mystical experience would have been dangerously unorthodox. Nevertheless, one has the impression, while reading certain Sufi texts, that their authors did in fact conceive of *al baqq,* the Real, as being the Divine Ground of Unity of Allah, underlying the active and personal aspects of Godhead.

The second doctrine of the Perennial Philosophy—that it is possible to know the Divine Ground by a direct intution higher than discursive reasoning—is to be found in all the great religions of the world. A philosopher who is content merely to know about the ultimate Reality—theoretically and by hearsay —is compared by Buddha to a herdsman of other men's cows. Mohammed uses an even homelier barn-yard metaphor. For him the philosopher who has not realized his metaphysics is just an ass bearing a load of books. Christian, Hindu and Taoist teachers write no less emphatically about the absurd pretensions of mere learning and analytical reasoning. In the words of the Anglican Prayer Book, our eternal life, now and hereafter, 'stands in the knowledge of God'; and this knowledge is not disursive but 'of the heart,' a super-rational intuition, direct, synthetic and timeless.

The third doctrine of the Perennial Philosophy, that which affirms the double nature of man is fundamental in all the higher religions. The unitive knowledge of the Divine Ground has, as its necessary condition, self-abnegation and charity. Only by means of self-abnegation and charity can we clear away the evil, folly and ignorance which constitute the thing we call our personality and prevent us from becoming aware of the spark of divinity illuminating the inner man. But the spark within is akin to the Divine Ground. By identifying ourselves with the first we can come to unitive knowledge of the second. These empirical facts of the spiritual life have been variously rationalized in terms of the theologies of the various religions. The Hindus categorically affirm that thou art That—that the indwelling Atman is the same as Brahman. For orthodox Christianity there is not an identity between the spark and God. Union of the human spirit with God takes place—union so complete that the word 'deification' is applied to it; but it is not the union of identical substances. According to the Christian theology, the saint is 'deified' not because Atman is Brahman, but because God has assimilated the purified human spirit into the divine substance by an act of grace. Islamic theology seems to make a similar distinction. The Sufi, Mansur, was executed for giving to the words 'union' and 'deification' the literal meaning which they bear in the Hindu tradition. For our present purposes, however the significant fact is that these words are actually used by Christians and Mohammedans to describe the empirical facts of metaphysical realization by means of direct, super-rational intuition.

In regard to man's final end, all the higher religions are in complete agreement. The purpose of human life is the discovery of Truth, the unitive knowledge of the Godhead.

The degree to which this unitive knowledge is achieved here on earth determines the degree, to which it will be enjoyed in the posthumous state. Contemplation of truth is the end, action the means. In India, in China, in ancient Greece, in Christian Europe, this was regarded as the most obvious and axiomatic piece or orthodoxy. The invention of the steam engine produced a revolution, not merely in industrial techniques, but also and much more significantly in philosophy. Because machines could be made progressively more and more efficient Western man came to believe that men and societies would automatically register a corresponding moral and spiritual improvement. Attention and allegiance came to be paid, not to Eternity, but to the Utopian future. External circumstances came to be regarded as more important than states of mind about external circumstances, and the end of human life was held to be action, with contemplation as a means to that end. These false and, historically aberrant and heretical doctrines are now systematically taught in our schools and repeated, day in day out, by those anonymous writers of advertising copy who, more than any other teachers, provide European and American adults with their current phiosophy of life. And so effective has been the propaganda that even professing Christians accept the heresy unquestioningly and are quite unconscious of its complete incompatibility with their own or anybody else's religion.

These four doctrines constitute the Perennial Philosophy in its minimal and basic form. A man who can practise what the Indians call Jnana yoga (the metaphysical discipline of discrimination between the real and the apparent) asks for nothing more. This simple working hypothesis is enough for his purposes. But such discrimination is exceedingly difficult and can hardly be practised, at any rate in the preliminary stages of the spiritual life, except by persons endowed with a particular kind of mental constitution. That is why most statements of the Perennial Philosophy have included another doctrine, affirming the existence of one or more human Incarnations of the Divine Ground, by whose meditation and grace the worshipper is helped to achieve his goal—that unitive knowledge of the Godhead, which is man's eternal life and beatitude. The Bhagavad Gita is one such statement.

Here Krishna is an Incarnation of the Divine Ground in human form. Similarly, in Christian and Buddhist theology, Jesus and Gautama are Incarntions of divinity. But whereas in Hinduism and Buddhism more than one Incarnation of the Godhead is possible (and is regarded as having in fact taken place), for Christians there has been and can be only one.

An Incarnation of the Godhead and, to a lesser degree, any theocentric saint, sage or prophet is a human being who knows Who he is and can therefore effectively remind other human beings of what they have allowed themselves to forget:

namely, that if they choose to become what potentially they already are, they too can be eternally united with the Divine Ground.

Worship of the Incarnation and contemplation of his attributes are for most men and women the best preparation for unitive knowledge of the Godhead. But whether the actual knowledge itself can be achieved by this means is another question. Many Catholic mystics have affirmed that, at a certain stage of that contemplative prayer in which, according in the most authoritative theologians, the life of Christian perfection ultimately "consists, it is necessary to put aside all thoughts of the Incarnations as distracting from the higher knowledge of that which has been incarnated. From this fact have arisen misunderstandings in plenty and a number of intellectual difficulties. Here, for example, is what Abbot John Chapman writes in one of his admirable Spiritual Letters. "The problem of *reconciling* (not merely uniting) mysticism with Christianity is more difficult. The Abbot (Abbot Marmion) says that St. John of the Cross is like a sponge full of Christianity. You can squeeze it all out, and the full mystical theory remains. Consequently fifteen years or so I hated St. John of the Cross and called him a Buddhist. I loved St. Teresa, and read her over and over again. She is first a Christian, only secondarily a mystic. Then I found that I had wasted fifteen years, so far as prayer was concerned." And yet, he concludes., in spite of its 'Buddhistic' character, the practice of mysticism (or, to put it in other terms, the realization of the Perennial Philosophy) makes good Christians. He might have added that it also makes good Hindus, good Buddhists, good Taoists, good Moslems and good Jews.

The solution to Abbot Chapman's problem must be sought in the domain, not of philosophy, but of psychology. Human beings are not born identical. There are many different temperaments and constitutions; and within each psychophysical class one can find people at very different stages of spiritual development. Forms of worship and spiritual discipline which may be valuable for one individual may be useless or even positively harmful for another belonging to a different class and standing, within that class, at a lower or higher level of development. All this is clearly set forth in the Gita where the psychological acts are linked up with general cosmology by means of the postulate of the *gunus.* Krishna, who is here the mouthpiece of Hinduism in all its manifestations, finds it perfectly natural that different men should have different methods and even apparently different objects of worship. All roads lead to Rome—provided, of course, that it is Rome and not some other city which the traveller really wishes to reach. A similar attitude of charitable inclusiveness, somewhat surprising in a Moslem, is beautifully expressed in the parable of Moses and the

Shepherd, told by Jalaluddin Rumi in the second book of the Masnavi. And within the more exclusive Christian tradition these problems of temperament and degree of development have been searchingly discussed in their relation to the way of Mary and the way of Martha in general, and in particular to the vocation and private devotions of individuals.

We now have to consider the ethical corollaries of the Perennial Philosophy."

"Truth" says St. Thomas Aquinas, "is the last end for the entire universe and the contemplation of truth is the chief occupation of wisdom." The moral virtues, he says in another place, belong in contemplation, not indeed essentially, but as a necessary pre-disposition. Virtue in other words is not the end but the indispensable means to the knowledge of Divine Reality. Shankara, the greatest of the Indian commentators on the Gita, holds the same doctrine. Right action is the way to knowledge; for it purifies the mind, and it is only to a mind purified from egotism that the intuition of the Divine Ground can come.

Self-abnegation, according to the Gita, can be achieved by the practice of two all-inclusive virtues—love and non-attachment. The latter is the same thing as that 'holy indifference,' on which St. Francois de Sales is never tired of insisting. "He who refers every action to God," writes Camus, summarizing his master's teaching, "and has no aims save His Glory, will find rest everywhere, even amidst the most violent commotions." So long as we practise this holy indifference to the fruits of action, "no lawful occupation will separate us from God; on the contrary, it can be made a means of closer union." Here the word 'lawful' supplies a necessary qualification to a teaching which, without it, is incomplete and 'even potentially dangerous.' Some actions are intrinsically evil or inexpedient; and no good intentions, no conscious offering of them to God, no renunciation of the fruits can alter their essential character. Holy indifference requires to be taught in conjunction not merely with a set of commandments prohibiting crimes, but also with a clear conception of what in Buddha's Eightfold Path is called 'right livelihood'. Thus, for the Buddhist right livelihood was incompatible with the making of deadly weapons and of intoxicants; for the mediaeval Christian, with the taking of interest and with various monopolistic practices which have since come to be regarded as legitimate good business. John Woolman, the American Quaker, provides a most enlightening example of the way in which a man may live in the world, while practising perfect non-attachment and remaining acutely sensitive to the claims of right livelihood. Thus, while it would have been profitable and perfectly lawful for him to sell West Indian sugar and rum to the customers who came to his shop, Woolman refrained from doing so because these things were the products of slave labour.

Similarly, when he was in England, it would have been both lawful and convenient for him to travel by stage-coach. Nevertheless, he preferred to make his journeys on foot. Why? Because the comforts of rapid travel could only be bought at the expense of great cruelty to the horses and the most atrocious working conditions for the post-boys. In Woolman's eyes, such a system of transportation was intrinsically undesirable, and no amount of personal non-attachment could make it anything but undesirable. So he shouldered his knapsack and walked.

In the preceding pages I have tried to show that the Perennial Philosophy and its ethical corollaries constitute a Highest Common Factor, present in all the major religions of the world. To affirm this truth has never been more imperatively necessary than at the present time. There will never be enduring peace unless and until human beings come to accept a' philosophy of life more adequate to the cosmic and psychological facts than the insane idolatries of nationalism and the advertising man's apocalyptic faith in Progress towards a mechanized New Jerusalem. All the elements of this philosophy are present, as we have seen, in the traditional religions. But in existing circumstances there is not the slightest chance that any of the traditional religions will obtain universal acceptance. Europeans and Americans will see no reason for being converted to Hinduism, say, or Buddhism. And the people of Asia can hardly be expected to renounce their own traditions for the Christianity professed, often sincerely by the imperialists who, for four hundred years and more, have been systematically attacking, exploiting and oppressing, and are now trying to finish off the work of destruction by 'educating' them. But happily there is the Highest Common Factor of all religions, the Perennial Philosophy which has always and everywhere been the metaphysical system of the prophets, saints and sages. It is perfectly possible for people to remain good Christians, Hindus, Buddhists or Moslems and yet to be united in full agreement on the basic doctrines of the Perennial Philosophy.

The Bhagavad Gita is perhaps the most systematic spiritual statement of the Perennial Philosophy. To a world at war, a world that, because it lacks the intellectual and spiritual prerequisites to peace, can only hope to patch up some kind of precarious armed truce, it stands pointing, clearly and unmistakably, to the only road of escape from the self-imposed necessity of self-destruction. For this reason we should be grateful to Swami Prabhavananda and Mr. Isherwood for having given us this new version of the book—a version which can be read, not merely without that dull aesthetic pain inflicted by all too many English translations from the Sanskrit, but positively with enjoyment.

ALDOUS HUXLEY

The Gita And War[1]

In the course of a year spent studying the Bhagavad-Gita, I have talked about its philosophy to a considerable number of people. Whatever else they had to say, I found them, almost without exception, agreed on one point: that the Gita 'sanctions' War. Some were glad of this. Others were sorry. But all, I think, were puzzled. Educated in the Christian tradition, they were accustomed to a gospel which is uncompromisingly pacifist. However deeply they might be convinced

1. Written in the year 1944.

of the justice or necessity of some particular conflict., they didn't like what they regarded as a general approval of the use of military force. They themselves, mere human beings struggling in the everyday world, might be driven to fight and kill one another, but they wanted Krishna, like Jesus, to stand for a higher ideal. That was their reaction.

I do not wish to sound superior or conceited when I say that I myself do not put this interpretation upon the teaching of the Gita. I will try to explain why I do not: not merely for the information of the few people who may be interested but because I want to straighten out my own ideas. The question is of the greatest importance to me, because I am myself a pacifist and because I believe the Gita to be one of the major religious documents of the world. If its teachings did not seem to agree with those of the other gospels and scriptures, then my own system of values would be thrown into confusion, and I should feel bewildered and unhappy.

Briefly, the circumstances of the Gita dialogue can be described as follows:

Two factions, closely bound to each other by ties of blood and friendship, are about to engage in a civil war. Arjuna, one of the leading generals, has Krishna for his charioteer. Krishna has told Arjuna that he will not fight, but has promised to accompany him throughout the battle. Just before it begins, Arjuna asks Krishna to drive his chariot into the no-man's-land between the two armies. Krishna does so. Arjuna looks at the opposing army, and realizes that he is about to kill those whom he loves better than life itself. In his despair he exclaims: "I will not fight!"

Krishna's reply to Arjuna occupies the rest of the book. It deals not only with Arjuna's immediate personal problem, but with the whole nature of action, the meaning of life, and the aims for which man must struggle, here on earth. Ai the end of their conversation, Arjuna has changed his mind. He is ready to fight. And the battle begins.

Before trying to analyse Krishna's arguments, I must mention two points which certain commentators have raised with regard to the battle itself. In the first place, it is sometimes said that the battle of Kurukshetra cannot possibly be compared to a battle in modern war. It was, in fact, a kind of tournament, governed by all the complex and human rules of ancient Indian chivalry. A soldier mounted upon an elephant may not attack a foot-soldier. No man may be struck or shot at while running away. No one may be killed who has lost his weapons. And we are told in the Mahabharata, that the opposing armies stopped fighting every evening, and even visited each other and fraternized during the night. In the second place, it is sometimes said that the whole battle is to be regarded allegorically. Arjuna is the individual man, Krishna is the indwelling Godhead, the enemies are man's evil tendencies, and so forth.

All this is interesting, of course. But it has nothing to do with our problem. If Krishna is only talking figuratively, or only about War under certain conditions, then the Gita is just a fable, an archaic curiosity: we need not discuss it. Personally I prefer to forget Kurukshetra and ancient India altogether, and imagine a similar dialogue taking place today, in a plane over the European front or the Japanese positions on a Pacific island. If the Gita has any validity, its reference is equally to this war and this very year.

To understand the Gita we must first consider what it is and what it is not. We must consider its setting. When Jesus spoke the words which are recorded as the Sermon on the Mount, he was talking to a group of followers in the most peaceful atmosphere imaginable, far from the great city, far from all strife and confusion. He was expressing the highest truth of which man's mind is capable, in general terms, without reference to any immediate crisis or problem. And even in the Garden of Gethsemane, when he told Peter to sheathe his sword, he was addressing a dedicated disciple, a monk, a man who was being trained to preach and live the spiritual life. For Peter, there could be no compromise. He must learn to accept the highest and strictest ideal, the ideal of non-violence.

The Gita is very different. Krishna and Arjuna are on a battlefield. Arjuna is a warrior by birth and profession. He corresponds to the mediaeval knight of Christendom. His problem is considered in relation to the circumstances of the moment. The Gita fits into the narrative of an epic poem, the Mahabharata, and must be read in the light of previous happenings. It is not simply a sermon, a philosophical treatise.

This, I believe, is the cause of much misunderstanding. We all tend to remember most clearly the part of a book which we read first. The opening chapters of the Gita deal with a particular case: they are concerned with a soldier and the duties of a soldier. Later on Krishna passes from the particular to the general, and utters those same truths which were afterwards taught by Jesus and the Buddha. But the first impression is apt to remain. The superficial reader closes the book and remembers only Arjuna and the battle. He says to himself: "Krishna tells us that we must fight."

Krishna, it must be repeated, is not talking to a monk. We ought to be glad of this, not sorry. The vast majority of mankind are not monks, but householders. What a great teacher has to say to a married man, a soldier, is of immediate interest to the world at large.

We must realize, also, that Krishna, in teaching Arjuna, employs two sets of values, the relative and the absolute. This duality is inherent in the circumstances of the story. For Krishna is both Arjuna's personal friend and his illumined teacher. He is a fellow-mortal and he is God. As God, he expresses the absolute truth, the highest ideal. As a fellow-man, he presents the relative values which apply to Arjuna's particular condition. Considered superficially, this duality of attitude may seem to produce contradictions. Carefully studied it will be seen to compose into a complete and satisfying philosophical picture. For life itself is double-faced; and any attempt at simplification will only bring us to ultimate confusion.

One circumstance renders Arjuna's compassion suspect: its occasion. Arjuna himself is dimly aware of this. "Is this real pity that I feel," he asks Krishna, "or only a delusion? My mind gropes about in darkness. I cannot see where my duty lies." Up to this moment Arjuna has not hesitated. He has accepted the necessity of the war. He has assumed responsibility for its leadership. Then, suddenly, he sees the other side of the picture: the bloodshed, the horror. And he recoils.

In the years that followed the 1914— 1918 war, much pacifist propaganda was based on gruesome narratives of battle and books of photographs showing mutilated corpses. "This is what War is like," said the authors. "Isn't it horrible? Do you want to go through this again?" And nearly everybody agreed that they didn't. But this sort of revulsion is always short-lived, because it appeals, fundamentally, to our cowardice. When a new war-situation develops, most of us react in the opposite direction, and rightly. Men can never, ultimately be deterred from any course of action by cowardice alone. Otherwise we should never have evolved from the jelly-fish. We have to go forward, and the path is always dangerous, in one way or another. Arjuna has to go forward. Krishna tells him so. Arjuna must accept the sum of his actions up to that moment—and the sum is this battle.

Krishna's reply begins by dealing with Arjuna's feelings of revulsion on general grounds. Arjuna shrinks from the act itself, the act of killing. Krishna reminds him that, in the absolute sense, there is no such act. The Atman, the indwelling Godhead, is the only reality. This body is simply an appearance: its existence, its destruction, are alike illusory. In the absolute sense, all talk of killing or being killed is meaningless.

"Some say this Atman
Is slain, and others
Call It the slayer:
They know nothing.
How can It slay
Or who shall slay It?"

Therefore, if Arjuna is objecting to the act of killing, as such, he need have no scruples. For he only seems to kill.

Then with one of those changes of viewpoint which may bewilder and shock a reader who opens the Gita for the first time and takes only its surface meaning. Krishna begins to talk to Arjuna as man to man:

Even if you consider this from the standpoint of your own caste-duty, you ought not to hesitate; for, to a warrior, there is nothing nobler than a righteous war...

"But if you refuse to fight this righteous war, you will be turning aside from your duty. You will be a sinner, and disgraced. People will speak ill of you throughout the ages...."

For Arjuna, a member of the warrior caste, the fighting of this battle, in defence of his family and property, is undoubtedly "righteous." It is his duty. In the Gita, we find that the caste-system is presented as a kind of natural order. Men are divided into four groups, according to their capacities and characteristics. Each group has its peculiar duties, ethics and responsibilities; and these must be accepted. It is the way of spiritual growth. A man must go forward from where he stands. He cannot jump to the Absolute: he must evolve towards it. He cannot arbitrarily assume the duties which belong to another group. If he does so, his whole system of values will be upset, his conscience can no longer direct him, and he will stray into pride or doubt or mental confusion. "Prefer to die doing your own duty," Krishna teaches. "The duty of another will bring you into great spiritual danger."

Socially, the caste-system is graded. The merchants are above the servants. The leaders and warriors are above the merchants. The priestly Brahmins are highest of all. But, spiritually there are no such distinctions. Krishna is very clear on this point. Everyone, he says, can attain the highest sainthood by following the prescribed path of his own caste-duty. In Southern India, we are told of seven saints who belonged to the lowest caste of all, the untouchables. And the same principle, of course, holds true if we apply the caste-classification to the social pattern of Europe. Men have grown into spiritual giants while carrying out their duties as merchants, peasants, doctors, popes, scullions or kings.

In the purely physical sphere of action, Arjuna is, indeed, no longer a free agent. The act of war is upon him: it has evolved out of his previous actions. He cannot choose. "If, in your vanity, you say 'I will not fight,' your resolve is vain. Your own nature will drive you to the act." At any given moment in time we are what we are; and our actions express that condition. We cannot run away from our actions, because we carry the condition with us. On the highest mountain, in the darkest cave, we must turn at last and accept the consequences of being ourselves. Only through this acceptance can we begin to evolve further. We may select the battleground. We cannot avoid the battle.

Arjuna is bound by the law of Karma, the law of cause and effect, which has brought him face to face with this particular situation. Now he is compelled to act, but he is still free to make his choice between two different ways of performing the action. Krishna introduces this great theme—the principal theme of the Gita—in the passage which immediately follows. He proceeds to define the nature of action.

In general, mankind almost always acts with attachment: that is to say, with fear and desire. Desire for a certain result and the fear that this result will not be obtained.

Attached action binds us to the world of appearance, to the continual doing of more action. We live in a delirium of doing and the consequences of our past actions condition the actions we are about to perform. According to the Gita, it is attached action which compels us to revisit this world, to be reborn again and again.

But there is another way of performing action; and this is without fear and without desire. The Christians call it holy indifference," and the Hindus 'non-attachment." Both names are slightly misleading. They suggest coldness and lack of enthusiasm. That is why people often confuse non-attachment with fatalism, when, actually, they are opposites. The fatalist simply does not care. He will get what is coming to him. Why make any effort? Fatalists are apt to get drunk or spend most of the day in bed. The doer of non-attached action, on the other hand, is the most conscientious of men. He does not run away from life: he accepts it much more completely than those whose pleasures are tinged with anxiety and whose defeats are embittered by regret. No matter whether he is sweeping out a room, or calculating the position of a star, or taking the chair at a meeting, he does it to the utmost limit of his powers—so carefully, so devotedly, so whole-heartedly, that the dividing-line between the chosen activity and the necessary chore disappears altogether. All work becomes equally and vitally important. It is only toward the results of work that he remains indifferent. Perhaps a dog runs across the clean floor with muddy paws. Perhaps his researches are recognized by Harvard University. Perhaps somebody throws a rotten egg at him. It doesn't matter. He goes right on with his job. We find something of this spirit in the lives of all truly great men and women, including the professed atheists and agnostics. Madame Curie refuses the Legion of Honor with the matter-of-fact words: "I don't see the utility of it." Lenin, in 1921, with the White armies converging on Moscow, his regime apparently doomed, work brought to nothing, calmly sits down and writes the order: "The peasants in the localities of Gorki and Zianova are immediately to be supplied with electric light." This, in its highest development, is the attitude of the saint. When action is done in this spirit, Krishna teaches, it will lead us to true wisdom, to the knowledge of what is behind action, behind all life: the ultimate Reality. And, with the growth of this knowledge, the need for further action will gradually fall away from us. The law of Karma will cease to operate. We shall realize our true nature, which is God.

It follows, therefore, that every action, under certain circumstances and for certain people may be a stepping-stone to spiritual growth—if it is done in the spirit of non-attachment. All good and evil is relative to the individual point of growth. For each Individual, certain acts are absolutely wrong. Indeed, there may well be acts which are absolutely wrong for every individual alive on earth today. But, in the highest sense, there can be neither good nor evil.

"The Lord is everywhere
And always perfect:
What does He care for man's sin
Or the righteousness of man?"

Because Krishna is speaking as God Himself, he can take this attitude, and advise Arjuna to fight. Because Arjuna has reached this particular stage in his development, he can kill his enemies and actually be doing his duty.

There is no question, here, of doing evil that good may come. The Gita does not countenance such opportunism. Arjuna is to do the best he knows, in order to pass beyond that best to better. Later, his fighting at Kurukshetra will seem evil to him, and it will be evil— then. Doing the evil you know to be evil will never bring good. It will lead only to more evil, more attachment, more ignorance.

How, in this complex world, are we to know what our own duty is? There is no greater problem. Yet, somehow, we have to find our position and make our stand. For the majority, much self analysis, much trial and error, would seem to be the only way. But having found that position, we must accept it in its entirety. The soldier has many responsibilities and duties besides fighting. The pacifist has much else to do besides refusing to fight. These duties and responsibilities extend equally over wartime and peace: they cover our whole life. But, in every case, the final ideal is the same.

The Gita neither sanctions war nor condemns it. Regarding no action as of absolute value, either for good or evil, it cannot possibly do either. Its teaching should warn us not to dare to judge others. How can we prescribe our neighbour's duty when it is so hard for us to know our own? The pacifist must respect Arjuna. Arjuna must respect the pacifist. Both are going towards the same goal; and only God can know which has made the greater progress. There is an underlying solidarity between them which can be expressed, if each one follows without compromise, the path upon which he finds himself. For we can only help others to do their duty by doing what we ourselves believe to be right. It is the one supremely social act.

Action rightly renounced brings
freedom:
Action rightly performed brings
freedom:
Both are better
Than mere shunning of action.
When a man lacks lust and hatred,
His renunciation does not waver.

He neither longs for one thing
Nor loathes its opposite:
The chains of his delusion
Are soon cast off.
The wise see knowledge and action
as one:
They see truly.
Take either path and tread it to
the end:
The end is the same.
There the followers of action
Meet the seekers after knowledge
In equal freedom.

—Bhagavad Gita

CHRISTOPHER ISHERWOOD

Gita And Mahabharata

The Mahabharata is said to be the longest poem in the world. In its original form, it consisted of twenty-four thousand verses, and it grew to about one hundred thousand. Like the Old Testament, it is not a homogeneous work, but a collection of narratives. Its central theme, as the name indicates, is the story of the descendants of King Bharata, (*Maha* means great) and of ancient India, the land where the Bharatas lived and ruled.

After the death of King Pandu, the Mahabharata tells us, how brother Dhritarashtra succeeded to the throne. Dhritarashtra educated the five sons of Pandu, the Pandavas, along with his own hundred sons. As they grew to be men, the pandavas distinguished themselves, by their piety and heroic virtues. In consequence, Duryodhana, Dhritarashtra's eldest son, became jealous and planned to murder them.

Duryodhana's scheme was to build a palace in a distant town, and invite the Pandavas to stay there during a religious festival. The palace was made of specially inflammable materials so that Duryodhana's servants could easily set it on fire. It burned to ashes but the Pandavas and Kunti, their mother, had been warned in time, and escaped. Duryodhana believed them dead.

The Pandavas lived in the forest, disguised as Brahmins, meeting all kinds of dangers and adventures. One day, they heard that a neighbouring king was to choose a husband for his daughter. The winner must bend a bow of enormous strength and hit a tiny target. The Pandavas thought they would try. They went in to the city in their disguise.

Suitors had gathered from all over India, Duryodhana among them. One after another, they failed in the test. At last Arjuna, third of the

Pandavas, stood up, bent the bow and hit the target with the greatest ease. Draupadi, the princess, threw him the victor's garland. But the assembled princes could not accept this humiliation at the hands of a seemingly poor and unwarlike Brahmin. There would have been a fight—just as in the story of Ulysses—if Krishna, who was present, had not intervened and persuaded them that Arjuna had a right to his bride. Krishna was a cousin of the Pandavas, but he was not one of Dhritarashtra's sons.

The brothers took Draupadi back to the forest, where Kunti was awaiting them. "Mother," they cried, "we have brought home a wonderful treasure!" "Be sure to share it equally, my children," Kunti answered; then she saw the girl, and exclaimed in dismay: "Oh, what have I said!" But it was too late. Her word was sacred to her sons. So Draupadi married all the brothers together.

Dhritarashtra and his sons now knew that the Pandavas were not only alive, but allied by marriage to a powerful monarch. Duryodhana was for carrying on the feud, but Dhritarashtra wisely listened to the advice of his uncle Bhishma, which was to send for the brothers and offer them half of his kingdom.

So the kingdom was divided. The Pandavas got the worst of the land, a wilderness along the Jamuna River. They cleared it, built a fine city, and crowned Yudhishthira. the eldest brother, as their king.

Now the five brothers lived in triumph and splendour, and Duryodhana hated them more than ever. He jealously hatched a new plot for their ruin. The pious and noble Yudhishthira had a dangerous weakness for gambling. So Duryodhana challenged him to play dice with a clever sharper named Sakuni, knowing that the king would feel bound in honour to accept. They played, sakuni cheated, Yudhishthira lost game after game, staking his wealth, his kingdom, and finally his brothers, Draupadi and himself. All were now the slaves of Duryodhana's vengeance, subject to insult and cruelty, until Dhritarashtra intervened, and insisted that they be set at liberty and their kingdom given back.

But Duryodhana worked upon his father until he obtained permission for another dice-match. The loser was to forfeit his kingdom and retire to the forest for twelve years, then he must live for a year in the city without being recognized; if he was discovered, the term of exile would begin again. This game also Yudhishthira lost. So the Pandavas went back to the forest. They made a virtue of their misfortune, practising spiritual austerities and doing many heroic deeds.

Once, during their wanderings, we are told, the brothers suffered greatly from thirst. Nakula was sent to look for water. He found a lake which was clear as crystal. As he bent over it, a voice said: "Stop, child. First answer my questions. Then you may drink." But Nakula, in his desperate thirst, paid no attention to the voice; he drank, and immediately fell dead.

His brother Sahadeva went out to look for him. He, too found the lake, and the same thing happened. In this manner, four of the Mothers died.

Last of all came Yudhishthira. He. found the corpses, and began to lament. Then the voice told him: "Child, first answer my questions, and then I will cure your grief and your thirst." He turned, and saw Dharma, the personification of duty and virtue, standing beside him in the form of a crane.

"What is the road to heaven?" the crane asked.

"Truthfulness."

"How does a man find happiness?"

"Through right conduct."

"What must he subdue, in order to escape grief?"

"His mind."

"When is a man loved?"

"When he is without vanity."

"Of all the world's wonders, which is the most wonderful?"

"That no man, though he sees others dying all around him, believes that he himself will die."

"How does one reach true religion?"

"Not by argument. Not by scriptures and doctrines; they cannot help. The path to religion is trodden by the saints."

Dharma was satisfied. He revealed himself to Yudhishthira. Then he brought the four brothers back to life.

When the period of exile was over at last, Yudhishthira asked for the return of his kingdom; but Duryodhana refused. Yudhishthira said he would be content with just one village for himself and for each of his brothers. But Duryodhana, in the insanity of his greed, would not agree even to this. The older members of the family tried to arbitrate, and failed. So war became inevitable. Neighbouring kings were drawn into the quarrel, until (In whole of India was involved. Both sides wanted Krishna's aid. To both, Krishna offered the same choice. "Either you can have the help of my kinsmen, the Vrishnis, in the battle," he told them, or you can have me, alone. But I shall take no part in the fighting." Duryodhana chose the Vrishnis. Arjuna preferred to take Krishna himself, as his personal charioteer.

The battle was fought on the plain of kurukshetra, a sacred place of pilgrimage. It was here, just before the armies engaged, that Krishna and Arjuna had the conversation which is recorded in the Bhagavad-Gita.

The battle lasted eighteen days, and ended with the death of Duryodhana and the complete victory of the Pandavas. Thereafter, Yudhishthira became undisputed ruler of India. He reigned for thirty-six years.

The story ends with the pilgrimage of Draupadi and the Pandavas up the heights of the Himalayas to the abode of God. On the way, the queen and four of the brothers died; they were not sufficiently pure to be able to enter heaven in their human bodies. Only Yudhishthira, the royal saint, journeyed on accompanied by his faithful dog. When they reached heaven, Indra, the king of the gods, told him that the dog could not come in. Yudhishthira replied that, if this was so, he would stay outside heaven too; for he could not bring himself to desert any creature which trusted him and wished for his protection. Finally, after a long argument, both dog and king were admitted. Then the dog was revealed as Dharma himself. This has been another test of Yudhishthira's spiritual greatness. One more was to follow. When the king looked around him, he found that heaven was filled with his mortal enemies. Where, he asked, were his brothers and his comrades?

Indra conducted him to a gloomy and horrible region, the pit of hell itself. "I prefer to stay here," said Yudhishthira, "for the place where they are is heaven to me." At this, the blackness horror vanished. Yudhishthira and the other Pandavas passed beyond the appearance of hell and heaven into the true Being of God which is immortality.

The Bhagavad-Gita (meaning, literally, the Song of God) is not regarded by Hindus as Sruti (scriptural teaching actually revealed by God to man, as in the Upanishads), but only as Smriti (the leaching of divine incarnations, saints or prophets, who further explain and elaborate the God-given truths of the scriptures). Nevertheless, it is the most popular book in Hindu religious literature: the Gospel, one may say of India. It has profoundly influenced the spiritual, cultural, intellectual and political life of the country throughout the centuries, and it continues to do so today. Every Westerner should study it, if he wants to understand the mental processes of India's thinkers and leaders.

The date of the Gita is generally placed by scholars somewhere between the fifth and second centuries, B.C. Most of them agree that it was not originally a part of the Mahabharata itself, but this does not necessarily mean that it was composed later than the epic. It seems to have existed for some time independently.

In the Gita dialogue there are four speakers: King Dhritarashtra, Sanjaya, Arjuna and Krishna.

Dhritarashtra is blind. The sage Vyasa (who is traditionally supposed to be the author of the Gita) offers to restore his sight, in order that he may watch the battle of Kuruskhetra. But Dhritarashtra refuses. He cannot bear to see his kinsmen killed. So Vyasa confers the psychic powers of clairvoyance and clairaudience upon Sanjaya, who is Dhritarashtra's minister and charioteer. As they sit together in the palace, Sanjaya describes to his master everything he sees and hears on the distant battle-field. Through his mouth, the words of Krishna and Arjuna are mediumistically reported. Occasionally, he pauses in this report to add descriptive remarks of his own.

Sri Krishna (*Sri* is a title of reverence, such as Lord) has been called the Christ of India. There are, in fact, some striking parallels between the life of Krishna, as related in the Bhagavatam and elsewhere and the life of Jesus of Nazareth. In both cases, legend and fact mingle; but the historical problem has nothing to do with a consideration of the message of the Bhagavad-Gita. To a seeker after spiritual reality who reads the Gita or the Sermon on the Mount, it cannot matter very much whether or not the historical Krishna and the historical Jesus ever existed at all.

The Gita is not primarily concerned with Krishna as an individual, but with his aspect as Brahman, the ultimate Reality. When Krishna addresses Arjuna, he sometimes speaks as an individual, but often as God Himself:

"For I am Brahman
Within this body,
Life immortal
That shall not perish;
I am the Truth
And the Joy forever."

Arjuna, in his attitude to Krishna, also expresses this dual relationship. Krishna is the divine incarnation of Vishnu, Arjuna's chosen deity. Arjuna knows this_yet, by a merciful ignorance, he sometimes forgets. Indeed, it is Krishna who makes him forget, since no ordinary man could bear the strain of constant companionship with God. After the vision of Krishna's divine aspect, which is recorded in chapter eleven, Arjuna is appalled by the realization that he has been treating the Lord of the universe as "friend and fellow-mortal." He humbly begs Krishna's pardon, but his awe soon leaves him. Again, he has forgotten. We may infer the same relationship between Jesus and his disciples after the vision of the transfiguration.

King Dhritarashtra speaks only once, In fact the whole narrative of the Gita is Sanjaya's answer to his single opening question.

CHAPTER I

The Sorrow Of Arjuna

Dhritarashtra: Tell me, Sanjaya what my sons and the sons of Pandu did, when they had gathered on the sacred field of Kurukshetra, eager for battle?

(In the following verses, Sanjaya describes how Duryodhana, seeing the opposing army of Pandavas in array, went to Drona, his teacher, and expressed his fear that their own army was the weaker of the two, although numerically larger. He named the leading warriors on either side. This is one of the catalogue-passages to be found in nearly all epics. It need not be translated in full.

In order to raise Duryodhana's failing courage, Bhishma, the commander-in-chief, sounded his conch-shell horn. But this was ill-advised—for the enemy chieftains immediately blew their horns in reply, and made much more noise. Their trumpeting "resounded through heaven and earth." we are told.

Arjuna now addresses Krishna, his friend and charioteer.

Arjuna:

Krishna the changeless,
Halt my chariot
There where the warriors,
Bold for the battle,
Face their foemen.
Between the armies
There let me see them,
The men I must fight with,
Gathered together
Now at the bidding
Of him their leader,
Blind Dhritarashtra's
Evil offspring:
Such are my foes
In the war that is coming.

Sanjaya (to *Dhritarashtra*) Then Krishna, subduer of the senses, thus requested by Arjuna, the conqueror of sloth,[1] drove that most splendid of chariots into a place between the two armies, confronting Bhishma, Drona and all those other rulers of the earth. And he said: "O Prince, behold the assembled Kurus!"

Then the prince looked on the array, and in both armies he recognized fathers and grandfathers, teachers, uncles, sons, brothers, grandsons, fathers-in-law, dear friends, and many other familiar faces.

---

1. Arjuna is traditionally supposed to have lived entirely without sleep. We may take this to mean that he had overcome all forms of laziness.

When Kunti's son saw all those ranks of kinsmen, he was filled with deep compassion, and he spoke despairingly, as follows:

Arjuna:

Krishna, Krishna.
Now as I look on
These my kinsmen
Arrayed for battle,
My limbs are weakened,
My mouth is parching,
My body trembles,
My hair stands upright,
My skin seems burning,
The bow Gandiva
Slips from my hand,
My brain is whirling

Round and round,
I can stand no longer:
Krishna, I see such
Omens of evil:
What can we hope from
This killing of kinsmen?
What do I want with
Victory, empire,
Or their enjoyment?
O Govinda,[1]
How can I care for
Power or pleasure,
My own life, even,
When all these others,
Teachers, fathers,
Grandfathers, uncles,
Sons and brothers,

---

1. One of the names of Sri Krishna, meaning Giver of Enlightenment.

Husbands of sisters,
Grandsons and cousins.
For whose sake only
I could enjoy them
Stand here ready
To risk blood and wealth
In war against us?
Knower of all things,
Though they should slay me
How could I harm them?
I cannot wish it:
Never, never,
Not though it won me
The throne of the three worlds;
How much the less for
Earthly lordship!

Krishna, hearing
The prayers of all men.

Tell me how can
We hope to be happy
Slaying the sons
of Dhritarashtra?
Evil they may be,
Worst of the wicked,
Yet if we kill them
Our sin is greater.
How could we dare spill
The blood that unites us?
Where is joy in
The killing of kinsmen?

Foul their hearts are
With greed, and blinded:
They see no evil
In breaking of blood-bonds.
See no sin
In treason to comrades.
But we, clear-sighted,

Scanning the ruin
Of families scattered,
Should we not shun
This crime, O Krishna?
We know what fate falls
On families broken:
The rites are forgotten,
Vice rots the remnant
Defiling the women.
And from their corruption
Comes mixing of castes:
The curse of confusion
Degrades the victims
And damns the destroyers.
The rice and the water
No longer are offered :
The ancestors also
Must fall dishonoured
From home in heaven.

Such is the crime
Of the killers of kinsmen:
The ancient, the sacred,
Is broken, forgotten.

Such is the doom
Of the lost, without caste-rites:
Darkness and doubting
And hell forever.
What is this crime
I am planning, O Krishna?
Murder most hateful,
Murder of brothers!
Am I indeed
So greedy for greatness?
Rather than this
Let the evil children
Of Dhritarashtra
Come with their weapons
Against me in battle:

I shall not struggle,
I shall not strike them.
Now let them kill me,
That will be better.

Sanjaya: Having spoken thus, Arjuna threw aside his arrows and his bow in the midst of the battle-field. He sat down on the seat of the chariot, and his heart was overcome with sorrow.

Chapter II

The Yoga Of Knowledge

Sanjaya: Then his eyes filled with tears, and his heart grieved and was be wildered with pity. And Sri Krishna spoke to him, saying:

Sri Krishna: Arjuna, is this hour of battle the time for scruples and fancies? Are they worthy of you, who seek enlightenment? Any brave man who merely hopes for fame or heaven would despise them.

What is this weakness? It is beneath you. Is it for nothing men call you the foe-consumer? Shake off this cowardice, Arjuna, stand up.

Arjuna: Bhishma and Drona are noble and ancient, worthy of the deepest reverence. How can I assail them with arrows, in battle? If I kill them, how can I ever enjoy my wealth, or any other pleasure? It will all be cursed with blood-guilt. I would much rather spare them, and eat the bread of a beggar.

Which will be worse, to win this war or to lose it? I scarcely know. Even the sons of Dhritarashtra stand in the enemy ranks. If we kill them, none of us will wish to live. Is this real pity that I feel, or only a delusion?

My mind gropes about in darkness. I cannot see where my duty lies. Krishna, I beg you, tell me frankly and clearly what I ought to do. I am your disciple. I put myself into your hands. Show me the way.

Not this world's kingdom,
Supreme, unchallenged,
No, nor the throne
Of the gods in heaven,
Could ease this sorrow
That numbs my senses!

Sanjaya: When Arjuna, the foe-consuming, the never-slothful, had spoken thus to Govinda, ruler of the senses, he added: "I will not fight," and was silent.

Then to him who thus sorrowed between the two armies, the ruler of the senses spoke, smiling:

Sri Krishna: Your words are wise, Arjuna, but your sorrow is for nothing. The truly wise mourn neither for the living nor for the dead.

There was never a time when I did not exist, nor you, nor any of these kings. Nor is there any future in which we shall cease to be.

Just as the dweller in this body passes through childhood, youth and old age, so at death he merely passes into another kind of body. The wise are not deceived by that.

Feelings of heat and cold, pleasure and pain, are caused by the contact of the senses with their objects. They come and they go, never lasting long. You must accept them.

A serene spirit accepts pleasure and pain with an even mind, and is unmoved by either. He alone is worthy of immortality.

That which is non-existent can never come into being, and that which is can never cease to be. Those who have known the inmost Reality know also the nature of *is* and *is not*.

That Reality which pervades the universe is indestructible. No one has power to change the Changeless.

Bodies are said to die, but That which possesses the body is eternal. It cannot be limited, or destroyed. Therefore you must fight.

Some say this Atman[1]
Is slain, and others
Call it the slayer:
They know nothing.
How can It slay
Or who shall slay It?

Know this Atman
Unborn, undying,
Never ceasing,
Never beginning,
Deathless, birthless,
Unchanging forever,
How can It die
The death of the body?

---

1. See Appendix

Knowing It birthless,
Knowing It deathless,
knowing It endless,
Forever unchanging,
Dream not you do
The deed of the killer,
Dream not the power
Is yours to command it.

Worn-out garments
Are shed by the body:
Worn-out bodies
Are shed by the dweller
Within the body:
New bodies are donned
By the dweller, like garments.

Not wounded by weapons,
Not burned by fire,
Not dried by the wind,
Not wetted by water:
Such is the Atman.

Not dried, not wetted,
Not burned, not wounded,
Innermost element,
Everywhere, always,
Being of beings,
Changeless, eternal,
For ever and ever.

This Atman cannot be manifested to the senses, or thought about by the mind. It is not subject to modification. Since you know this, you should not grieve, But if you should suppose this Atman to be subject to constant birth and death, even then you ought not to be sorry. Death is certain for the born. Rebirth is certain for the dead. You should not grieve for what is unavoidable.

Before birth, beings are not manifest to our human senses. In the interim between birth and death, they are manifest. At death they return to the unmanifest again. What is there in all this to grieve over?

There are some who have actually looked upon the Atman, and understood It, in all Its wonder. Others can only speak of It as wonderful beyond their understanding. Others know of Its wonder by hearsay. And there are others who are told about It, and do not understand a word.

He Who dwells within all living bodies remains forever indestructible.

Therefore, you should never mourn for anyone.

Even if you consider this from the standpoint of your own caste-duty, you ought not to hesitate; for, to a warrior, there is nothing nobler than a righteous war. Happy are the warriors to whom a battle such as this comes; it opens a door to heaven. But if you refuse to fight this righteous war, you will be turning aside from your duty. You will be a sinner, and disgraced. People will speak ill of you throughout the ages. To a man who values his honour, that is surely worse than death. The warrior-chiefs will believe it was fear that drove you from the battle; you will be despised by those who have admired you so long. Your enemies also, will slander your courage. They will use the words which should never be spoken. What could be harder to bear than that?

Die, and you win heaven. Conquer, and you enjoy the earth. Stand up now, son of Kunti, and resolve to fight. Realize that pleasure and pain, gain and loss, victory and defeat, are all one and the same: then go into battle. Do this and you cannot commit any sin.

I have explained to you the true nature of the Atman. Now listen to the method of Karma Yoga.[1] If you can understand and follow it, you will be able to break the chains of desire which bind you to your actions.

In this yoga, even abortive attempt is not wasted. Nor can it

---

1. Karma: (1) Work, a deed.
(2) Effect of a deed.
(3) Law of causation governing action and its effects in the Physical and Psychological planes.

Yoga: (1) Union with God.
(2) A prescribed path of spiritual life. The various yogas are therefore, different paths to union with God. Karma Yoga is the path of selfless God-dedicated action.

Yogi : One who practises yoga.

produce a contrary result. Even a little practice of this yoga will save you from the terrible wheel of rebirth and death.

In this yoga, the will is directed singly toward one ideal. When a man lacks this discrimination, his will wanders in all directions, after innumerable aims. Those who lack discrimination may quote the letter of the scripture, but they are really denying its inner truth. They are full of worldly desires, and hungry for the rewards of heaven. They use beautiful figures of speech. They teach elaborate rituals which are supposed to secure pleasure and power for those who perform them. But, actually, they understand nothing except the law of Karma, that chains men to rebirth.

Those whose discrimination is stolen away by such talk grow deeply attached to pleasure and power. And so they are unable to develop that concentration of the will which leads a man to absorption in God.

The Vedas[1] teach us about the three gunas[2] and their functions. You, Arjuna, must overcome the three

1. Revealed sciptures of the Hindus. The reference here is for the ritualistic portion of the Vedas.

2. See Appendix.

gunas. You must be free from the pairs of opposites.[1] Poise your mind in tranquility. Take care neither to acquire nor to hoard. Be established in the consciousness of the Atman, always.

When the whole country is flooded, the reservoir becomes superfluous. So, to the illumined seer, the Vedas are all superfluous.

You have the right to work, but for work's sake only. You have no right to the fruits of work. Desire for the fruits of work must never be your

1. Heat and cold, pleasure and pain. etc. The seeming contradictions of the relative world.

motive in working. Never give way to laziness, either.

Perform every action with your heart fixed on the Supreme Lord. Renounce attachment to the fruits. Be even-tempered in success and failure; for it is this evenness of temper which is meant by yoga.

Work done with anxiety about results is far inferior to work done without such anxiety, in the calm of self-surrender. Seek refuge in the knowledge of Brahman.[1] They who work selfishly for results are miserable.

In the calm of self-surrender you can free yourself from the bondage

1. See Appendix.

of virtue and vice during this very life. Devote yourself, therefore, to reaching union with Brahman. To unite the heart with Brahman and then to act: that is the secret of non-attached work. In the calm of self-surrender, the seers renounce the fruits of their actions, and so reach enlightenment. Then they are free from the bondage of rebirth, and pass to that state which is beyond all evil.

When your intellect has cleared itself of its delusions you will become indifferent to the results of all action, present in future. At present your intellect is bewildered by conflicting interpretations of the scriptures. When it can rest, steady and undistracted, in contemplation of the Atman, then you will reach union with the Atman.

Arjuna: Krishna, how can one identify a man who is firmly established and absorbed in Brahman? In what manner does an illumined soul speak? How does he sit? How does he walk?

Sri Krishna:

He knows bliss in the Atman
And wants nothing else.
Cravings torment the heart:
He renounces cravings.
I call him illumined.

Not shaken by adversity,
Not hankering after happiness:
Free from fear, free from anger,
Free from the things of desire:
I call him a seer, and illumined.

The bonds of his flesh are broken.
He is lucky, and does not rejoice:
He is unlucky, and does not weep.
I call him illumined.

The tortoise can draw in its legs:
The seer can draw in his senses.
I call him illumined.

The abstinent run away from
what they desire,
But carry their desires with them:
When a man enters Reality,
He leaves his desires behind him.
Even a mind that knows the path

Can be dragged from the path:
The senses are so unruly.

But he controls the senses
And recollects the mind
And fixes it on Me.
I call him illumined.

Thinking about sense-objects
Will attach you to sense-objects;
Grow attached, and you become addicted;
Thwart your addiction, it turns to anger;
Be angry, and you confuse your mind;
Confuse your mind, you forget the lesson of experience:
Forget experience, you lose discrimination,

Lose discrimination, and you miss
life's only purpose.

When he has no lust, no hatred.
A man walks safely among
the things of lust and hatred.
To obey the Atman
Is his peaceful joy:
Sorrow melts
Into that clear peace:
His quiet mind
Is soon established in peace.

The uncontrolled mind
Does not guess that the Atman is
present:
How can it meditate?
Without meditation, where is peace?
Without peace, where is happiness?
The wind turns a ship

From its course upon the waters:
The wandering winds of the senses
Cast man's mind adrift
And turn his better judgment from
its course.
When a man can still the senses
I call him illumined.

The recollected mind is awake
In the knowledge of the Atman
Which is dark night to the ignorant:
The ignorant are awake in their
sense-life
Which they think is daylight:
To the seer it is darkness.
Water flows continually into the ocean
But the ocean is never disturbed:
Desire flows into the mind of the seer
But he is never disturbed.

The seer knows peace:
The man who stirs up his own lusts
Can never know peace.
He knows peace who has forgotten desire.
He lives without craving:
Free from ego, free from pride.
This is the state of enlightenment in Brahman:
A man does not fall back from it
Into delusion.
Even at the moment of death
He is alive in the enlightenment:
Brahman and he are one.

Chapter III

Karma Yoga

Arjuna: But, Krishna, if you consider knowledge of Brahman superior to any sort of action, why are You telling me to do these terrible deeds?

Your statements seem to contradict each other. They confuse my mind. Tell me one definite way of reaching the highest good.

Sri Krishna: I have already told you that, in this world, aspirants may find enlightenment by two different paths. For the contemplative is the path of knowledge: for the active is the path of selfless action.

Freedom from activity is never achieved by abstaining from action. Nobody can become perfect by merely ceasing to act. In fact, nobody can ever rest from his activity[1] even for a moment. All are helplessly forced to act, by the gunas.

A man who renounces certain physical actions but still lets his mind dwell on the objects of his sensual desire, is deceiving himself. He can only be called a hypocrite. The truly admirable man controls his

1. Here "activity" includes mental action, conscious and sub-conscious.

senses by the power of his will. All his actions are disinterested. All are directed along the path to union with Brahman.

Activity is better than inertia. Act, but with self-control. If you are lazy, you cannot even sustain your own body.

The world is imprisoned in its own activity, except when actions are performed as worship of God. Therefore you must perform every action sacramentally, and be free from all attachment to results.

In the beginning
The lord of beings
Created all men,

To each his duty.
"Do this," He said,
"And you shall prosper.
Duty well done
Fulfils desire
Like Kamadhenu[1]
The wish-fulfiller."

"Doing of duty
Honours the devas
To you the devas[2]
In turn will be gracious:
Each honouring other,
Man reaches the Highest.

Please the devas:
Your prayer will be granted."
But he who enjoys the devas' bounty

---

1. A legendary cow, mentioned in the Mahabharata.
2. The inhabitants of heaven.

Showing no thanks,
He thieves from the devas.

Pious men eat
What the gods leave over
After the offering:
Thus they are sinless.

But those ungodly,
Cooking good food
For the greed of their stomachs,
Sin as they eat it.
Food quickens the life-sperm:
Food grows from the rainfall
Called down out of heaven
By sacrifice offered :
Sacrifice speaks
Through the act of the ritual.

This is the ritual
Taught by the sacred
Scriptures that spring

From the lips of the Changeless:
Know therefore that Brahman
The all-pervading
Is dwelling forever
Within this ritual.
If a man plays no part
In the acts thus appointed
His living is evil;
His joy is in lusting.
Know this, O Prince:
His life is for nothing.

But when a man has found delight and satisfaction and peace in the Atman, then he is no longer obliged to perform any kind of action. He has nothing to gain in this world by action, and nothing to lose by refraining from action. He is independent of everybody and everything. Do your duty, always; but without attachment. That is how a man reaches the ultimate truth; by working without anxiety about results. In fact, Janaka[1] and many others reached enlightenment, merely by doing their duly in this spirit. Your motive in working should be to set others, by your example on the path of duty.

Whatever a great man does, ordinary people will imitate; they follow his example. Consider me: I am not bound by any sort of duty. There is nothing, in all the three worlds which I do not already possess;

---

1. A royal saint mentioned in the Upanishads.

nothing I have yet to acquire. But I go on working, nevertheless. If I did not continue to work untiringly as I do, mankind would still follow me, no matter where I led them. Suppose I were to stop? They would all be lost. The result would be caste-mixture and universal destruction.

The ignorant work
For the fruit of their action:
The wise must work also
Without desire
Pointing man's feet
To the path of his duty.
Let the wise beware
Lest they bewilder
The minds of the ignorant
Hungry for action.
Let them show by example

How work is holy
When the heart of the worker
Is fixed on the Highest.

Every action is really performed by the gunas. Man, deluded by his egoism, thinks: "I am the doer." But he who has true insight into the operations of the gunas and their various functions, knows that when senses attach themselves to objects, gunas are merely attaching themselves to gunas. Knowing this, he does not become attached to his actions.

The illumined soul must not create confusion in the minds of the ignorant by refraining from work. The ignorant, in their delusion, identify the Atman with the gunas. They become tied to the senses and the action of the senses.

Shake off this fever of ignorance. Stop hoping for worldly rewards. Fix your mind on the Atman. Be free from the sense of ego. Dedicate all your actions to me. Then go forward and fight.

If a man keeps following my teaching with faith in his heart, and does not make mental reservations, he will be released from the bondage of his karma. But those who scorn my teaching, and do not follow it, are lost. They are without spiritual discrimination. All their knowledge is a delusion.

Even a wise man acts according to the tendencies of his own nature. All living creatures follow their tendencies. What use is any external restraint? The attraction and aversion which the senses feel for the different objects are natural. But you must not give way to such feeling; they are obstacles.

It is better to do your own duty, however imperfectly, than to assume the duties of another person, however successfully. Prefer to die doing your own duty: the duty of another will bring you into great spiritual danger.

Arjuna: Krishna, what is it that makes a man do evil, even against his own will; under compulsion, as it were?

Sri Krishna: The rajo-guna[1] has two faces, rage and lust; the ravenous, the deadly: Recognize these: they are your enemies.

Smoke hides fire,
Dust hides a mirror,
The womb hides the embryo:
By lust the Atman is hidden.
Lust hides the Atman in its hungry
flames,
The wise man's faithful foe.

Intellect, senses and mind
Are fuel to its fire:
Thus it deludes
The dweller in the body.
Bewildering his judgment.

1. See Appendix.

Therefore, Arjuna, you must first control your senses, then kill this evil thing which obstructs discriminative knowledge and realization of the Atman.

The senses are said to be higher than the sense-objects. The mind is higher than the senses. The intelligent will is higher than the mind. What is higher than the intelligent will? The Atman Itself.

You must know Him who is above the intelligent will. Get control of the mind through spiritual discrimination. Then, destroy your elusive enemy, who wears the form of lust.

CHAPTER IV

Renunciation Through Knowledge

Sri Krishna:

Foe-consumer,
Now I have shown you
Yoga that leads
To the truth undying.
I taught this yoga
First to Vivaswat,
Vivaswat taught it
In turn to Manu,
Next Ikshvaku
Learnt it from Manu,
And so the sages
In royal succession
Carried it onward

From teacher to teacher,
Till at length it was lost,
Throughout ages forgotten.

Arjuna: Vivaswat was born long before you. How am I to believe that you were the first to teach this yoga?

Sri Krishna:

You and I, Arjuna,
Have lived many lives.
I remember them all:
You do not remember.

I am the birthless, the deathless,
Lord of all that breathes.
I seem to be born:
It is only seeming,
Only my Maya.[1]

1. See Appendix

I am still master
Of my Prakriti.
The power that makes me.

When goodness grows weak,
When evil increases,
I make myself a body.

In every age I come back
To deliver the holy,
To destroy the sin of the sinner
To establish righteousness.

He who knows the nature
Of my task and my holy birth
Is not reborn
When he leaves this body:
He comes to me.
Flying from fear,
From lust and anger,
He hides in me,

His refuge, his safety:
Burnt clean in the blaze of
my being.
In me many find home.

Whatever wish men bring me in
worship,
That wish I grant them.
Whatever path men travel
Is my path:
No matter where they walk
It leads to me.

Most men worship the gods because they want success in their wordly undertakings. This kind of material success can be gained very quickly, here on earth.

I established the four castes, which correspond to the different types of guna and karma. I am their author; nevertheless, you must realize that I am beyond action and changeless. Action does not contaminate me. I have no desire at all for the fruits of action. A man who understands my nature in this respect will never become the slave of his own activity. Because they understood this, the ancient seekers for liberation could safely engage in action. You, too, must do your work in the spirit of those early seers.

What is action? What is inaction? Even the wise are puzzled by this question. Therefore, I will tell you what action is. When you know that, you will be free from all impurity. You must learn what kind of work to do, what kind of work to avoid, and how to reach a state of calm detachment from your work. The real nature of action is hard to understand.

He who sees the inaction that is in action and the action that is in inaction, is wise indeed. Even when he is engaged in action, he remains poised in the tranquillity of the Atman.

The seers say truly
That he is wise
Who acts without lust or scheming
For the fruit of the act:
Its chain is broken,

His act falls from him,
Melted in the flame of my
knowledge.

Turning his face from the fruit,
He needs nothing:
The Atman is enough.
He acts, and is beyond action.

Not hoping, not lusting,
Bridling body and mind,
He calls nothing his own:
He acts, and earns no evil.

What God's Will gives
He takes, and is contented.
Pain follows pleasure,
He is not troubled:
Gain follows loss,
He is indifferent:
Of whom should he be jealous?

He acts, and is not bound by his
action.

When the bonds are broken
His illumined heart
Beats in Brahman:
His every action
Is worship of Brahman:
Can such acts bring evil?

Brahman is the ritual,
Brahman is the offering,
Brahman is he who offers
To the fire that is Brahman.
If a man sees Brahman
In every action,
He will find Brahman.[1]

1. The verse is chanted by all Hindu monks as a grace before meals. In this case "the fire" is regarded as the fire of hunger.

Some yogis merely worship the devas. Others are able, by the grace of the Atman, to meditate on the identity of the Atman with Brahman. For these, the Atman is the offering, and Brahman the sacrificial fire into which It is offered.

Some withdraw all their senses from contact with exterior sense-objects. For these, hearing and the other senses are the offering, and self-discipline the sacrificial fire. Others allow their minds and senses to wander unchecked, and try to see Brahman within all exterior sense-objects. For these, sound and the other sense-objects are the offering, and sense-enjoyment the sacrificial fire.

Some renounce all the actions of the senses, and all the functions of the vital force. For these, such actions and functions are the offering, and the practice of self-control is the sacrifial fire, kindled by knowledge of the Atman.

Then there are others whose way of worship is to renounce sense-objects and material possessions. Others set themselves austerities and spiritual disciplines: that is their way of worship. Others worship through the practice of Raja Yoga.[1] Others who are earnest seekers for perfection and men of strict vows, study and meditate on the truths of scriptures. That is their way of worship.

Others are intent on controlling the vital energy; so they practise breathing-exercises — inhalation,

---

1. The Path of Raja Yoga is said to have eight steps: (1) Practice of the moral virtues, (2) Regular habits of purity, contentment, study, austerity and self-surrender to God. (3) Posture. (4) Control of the vital energy by breathing-exercises. (5) Withdrawal of the mind from sense-objeets. (6) Concentration. (7) Meditation. (8) Absorption in the consciousness of God.

exhalation, and the stoppage of the breath. Others mortify their flesh by fasting, to weaken their sensual desires, and thus achieve self-control.

All these understand the meaning of sacrificial worship. Through worship, their sins are consumed away. They eat the food which has been blessed in the sacrifice. Thus they obtain immortality and reach eternal Brahman. He who does not worship God cannot be happy even in this world. What, then, can he expect from any other?

All these, and many other forms of worship are prescribed by the scriptures.

All of them involve the doing of some kind of action. When you fully understand this, you will be made free in Brahman.

The form of worship which consists in contemplating Brahman is superior to ritualistic worship with material offerings.

The reward of all action is to be found in enlightenment.

Those illumined souls who have realized the Truth will instruct you in the knowledge of Brahman, if you prostrate yourself before them, question them and serve them as a disciple.

When you have reached enlightenment, ignorance will delude you no longer. In the light of that knowledge, you will see the entire creation within your own Atman and in me.

And though you were the foulest of
sinners.
This knowledge alone would carry you
Like a raft, over all your sin.

The blazing fire turns wood to ashes:
The fire of knowledge turns all
karmas to ashes.
On earth there is no purifier
As great as this knowledge.
When a man is made perfect in yoga,
He knows its truth within his heart.

The man of faith,
Whose heart is devoted,
Whose senses are mastered,
He finds Brahman.
Enlightened, he passes
At once to the highest,
The peace beyond passion.

The ignorant, the faithless, the doubter
Goes to his destruction.
How shall he enjoy
This world, or the next,
Or any happiness?

When a man can act without desire,
Through practice of yoga,
When his doubts are torn to shreds,
Because he knows Brahman;
When his heart is poised
In the being of the Atman
No bonds can bind him.

Still I can see it:
A doubt that lingers
Deep in your heart
Brought forth by delusion,
You doubt the truth
Of the living Atman.

Where is your sword
Discrimination?
Draw it and slash
Delusion to pieces.
Then arise O son of Bharata:
Take your stand
In Karma Yoga.

Chapter V

The Yoga Of Renunciation

Arjuna: You speak so highly of the renunciation of action; yet you ask me to follow the yoga of action. Now tell me definitely: which of these is better?

Sri Krishna:

Action rightly renounced brings
freedom:
Action rightly performed brings
freedom:
Both are better
Than mere shunning of action.

When a man lacks lust and hatred,
His renunciation does not waver.
He neither longs for one thing
Nor loathes its opposite;
The chains of his delusion
Are soon cast off.

The yoga of action, say the ignorant,
Is different from the yoga of the
knowledge of Brahman.
The wise see knowledge and action
as one:
They see truly.
Take either path
And tread it to the end:
The end is the same.
There the followers of action
Meet the seekers after knowledge
In equal freedom.

It is hard to renounce action
Without following the yoga of action.
This yoga purifies
The man of meditation,
Bringing him soon to Brahman,
When the heart is made pure
by that yoga,
When the body is obedient,
When the senses are mastered,
When man knows that his Atman
Is the Atman in all creatures,
Then let him act,
Untainted by action.

The illumined soul
Whose heart is Brahman's heart
Thinks always: "I am doing nothing."
No matter what he sees,
Hears, touches, smells, eats;
No matter whether he is moving,

Sleeping, breathing, speaking,
Excreting, or grasping something
with his hand,
Or opening his eyes,
Or closing his eyes:
This he knows always:
"I am not seeing, I am not hearing:
It is the senses that see and hear
And touch the things of the senses.'

He puts aside desire,
Offering the act to Brahman.
The lotus leaf rests unwetted by
water:
He rests on action, untouched by
action.

To the follower of the yoga of action,
The body and the mind,
The sense-organs and the intellect

Are instruments only:
He knows himself other than the
instrument
And thus his heart grows pure.

United with Brahman,
Cut free from the fruit of the act,
A man finds peace
In the work of the spirit.
Without Brahman,
Man is a prisoner,
Enslaved by action,
Dragged onward by desire.

Happy is that dweller
In the city of nine gates[1]
Whose discrimination
Has cut him free from his act:

---

1. The human body.

He is not involved in action,
He does not involve others.

Do not say:

"God gave us this delusion."
You dream you are the doer,
You dream that action is done,
You dream that action bears fruit.
It is your ignorance,

It is the world's delusion
That gives you these dreams.

The Lord is everywhere
And always perfect:
What does He care for man's sin
Or the righteousness of man?
The Atman is the light:
The light is covered by darkness:
This darkness is delusion:
That is why we dream.

When the light of the Atman
Drives out our darkness,
That light shines forth from us,
A sun in splendour,
The revealed Brahman.

The devoted dwell with Him.
They know Him always
There in the heart,
Where action is not.
He is all their aim.
Made free by His Knowledge

From past uncleanness
Of deed or of thought,
They find the place of freedom,
The place of no return.[1]

---

1. The state in which one is no longer subject to rebirth, because illumination has been attained.

Seeing all things equal,
The enlightened may look
On the Brahmin, learned and gentle,
On the cow, on the elephant,
On the dog, on the eater of dogs.

Absorbed in Brahman
He overcomes the world
Even here, alive in the world.
Brahman is one.
Changeless, untouched by evil:
What home have we but Him?
The enlightened, the Brahman
abiding.
Calm-hearted, unbewildered,
Is neither elated by the pleasant
Nor saddened by the unpleasant.

His mind is dead
To the touch of the external:

It is alive
To the bliss of the Atman.
Because his heart knows Brahman
His happiness is for ever.

When senses touch objects
The pleasures therefrom
Are like wombs that bear sorrow.
They begin, they are ended:
They bring no delight to the wise.
Already, here on earth,
Before his departure,
Let man be the master
Of every impulse
Lust-begotten
Or fathered by anger:
Thus he finds Brahman,
Thus he is happy.
Only that yogi
Whose joy is inward,

Inward his peace,
And his vision inward
Shall come to Brahman
And know Nirvana.[1]

All consumed
Are their imperfections,
Doubts are dispelled,
Their senses mastered,
Their every action
Is wed to the welfare
Of fellow-creatures :
Such are the seers
Who enter Brahman
And know Nirvana.
Self-controlled,
Cut free from desire,
Curbing the heart

1. The state of union with Brahman.

And knowing the Atman,
Man finds Nirvana
That is in Brahman,
Here and hereafter.

Shutting off sense
From what is outward,
Fixing the gaze
At the root of the eye-brows,[1]
Checking the breath-stream
In and outgoing
Within the nostrils,
Holding the senses,
Holding the intellect,
Thrusts fear aside,

---

1. "When the eyes are half closed in meditation the eyeballs remain fixed and their gaze converges, as it were, between the eyebrows."

—Swami Swarupananda.

Thrusts aside anger
And puts off desire:
Truly that man
Is made free forever.

When thus he knows me
The end, the author
Of every offering
And all austerity,
Lord of the worlds
And the friend of all men:
O son of Kunti,
Shall he not enter
The peace of my presence?

CHAPTER VI

The Yoga Of Meditation

Sri Krishna:

He who does the task
Dictated by duty,
Caring nothing
For fruit of the action,
He is a Yogi,
A true sannyasin.[1]
But he who follows
His vow to the letter
By mere refraining:

Lighting no fire
At the ritual offering,
Making excuse

1. Sannyasin; A monk.

For avoidance of labour.
He is no Yogi,
No true sannyasin.

For he must understand that what has been called yoga is really sannyasa[1], since nobody can practise the yoga of action who is anxious about his future, or the results of his actions.

Let him who would climb
In meditation
To heights of the highest
Union with Brahman
Take for his path

---

1. Sannyasa; The formal vow of renunciation taken by a monk. In taking this vow, he gives up the performance of Vedic sacrificial rites.

The yoga of action:
Then when he nears
That height of oneness
His acts will fall from him,
His path will be tranquil.

For when a man loses attachment to sense-objects and to action, when he renounces lustful anxiety and anxious lust, then he is said to have climbed to the height of union with Brahman.

What is man's will
And how shall he use it?
Let him put forth its power
To uncover the Atman
Not hide the Atman:
Man's will is the only
Friend of the Atman:

His will is also
The Atman's enemy.

For when a man is self-controlled, his will is the Atman's friend. But the will of an uncontrolled man is hostile to the Atman, like an enemy.

That serene one
Absorbed in the Atman
Masters his will,
He knows no disquiet
In heat or in cold,
In pain or in pleasure,
In honour, dishonour.

For when a man's heart has reached fulfillment through knowledge and personal experience of the truth of Brahman he is never again moved by the things of the senses. Earth, stone and gold seem all alike to one who has mastered one's senses. Such a yogi is said to have achieved union with Brahman.

He who regards
With an eye that is equal
Friends and comrades,
The foe and the kinsman,
The vile, wicked,
The men who judge him,
And those who belong
To neither faction:
He is the greatest.

The Yogi should retire into a solitary place, and live alone. He must exercise control over his mind and body. He must free himself from the hopes and possessions of this world. He should meditate on the Atman unceasingly.

The place where he sits should be firm, neither too high nor too low, and situated in a clean spot. He should first cover it with sacred grass, then with a deer skin; then lay a cloth over these.[1] As he sits there, he is to hold the senses and imagination in check, and keep the mind concentrated upon its object. If he practises meditation in this manner, his heart will become pure.

1. The choice of material is traditional, but not important for the spiritual aspirant of to-day. Any convenient seat will do.

His posture must be motionless, with the body, head and neck held erect, and the vision indrawn, as if gazing at the tip of the nose. He must not look about him.

So, with his heart serene and fearless,
Firm in the vow of renunciation,
Holding the mind from its restless
roaming.
Now let him struggle to reach
my oneness,
Ever-absorbed, his eyes on me always,
His prize, his purpose.

If a yogi has perfect control over his mind, and struggles continually in this way to unite himself with Brahman, he will come at last to the crowning peace of Nirvana, the peace that is in me.

Yoga is not for the man who overeats, or for him who fasts excessively. It is not for him who sleeps too much, or for the keeper of exaggerated vigils. Let a man be moderate in his eating and his recreation, moderately active, moderate in sleep and in wakefulness. He will find that yoga takes away all his unhappiness.

When can a man be said to have achieved union with Brahman? When his mind is under perfect control and freed from all desires, so that he becomes absorbed in the Atman, and nothing else. "The light of a lamp does not flicker in a windless place": that is the simile which describes a Yogi of one-pointed mind, who meditates upon the Atman. When, through the practice of yoga, the mind ceases its restless movements, and becomes still, he realizes the Atman. It satisfies him entirely. Then he knows that infinite happiness which can be realized by the purified heart but is beyond the grasp of the senses. He stands firm in this realization. Because of it, he can never again wander from the inmost truth of his being.

Now that he holds it
He knows this treasure

Above all others:
Faith so certain
Shall never be shaken
By heaviest sorrow.

To achieve this certainty is to know the real meaning of the word yoga. It is the breaking of contact with pain. You must practise this yoga resolutely, without losing heart. Renounce all your desires, forever. They spring from wilfulness. Use your discrimination to restrain the whole pack of the scattering senses.

Patiently, little by little, a man must free himself from all mental distractions, with the aid of the intelligent will. He must fix his mind upon the Atman, and never think of anything else. No matter where the restless and unquiet mind wanders, it must be drawn back and made to submit to the Atman only.

Utterly quiet.
Made clean of passion,
The mind of the yogi
Knows that Brahman,
His bliss is the highest.
Released from evil
His mind is constant
In contemplation:
The way is easy,
Brahma has touched him,
That bliss is boundless.

His heart is with Brahman,
His eye in all things

Sees only Brahman
Equally present,
Knows his own Atman
In every creature,
And all creation
Within that Atman.

That yogi sees me in all things, and all things within me. He never loses sight of me, nor I of him. He is established in union with me, and worships me devoutly in all beings. That yogi abides in me, no matter what his mode of life.

Who burns with the bliss
And suffers the sorrow
Of every creature
Within his own heart,
Making his own

Each bliss and each sorrow:
Him I hold highest
Of all the yogis.

Arjuna: Krishna, you describe this yoga as a life of union with Brahman. But I do not see how this can be permanent. The mind is so very restless.

Restless man's mind is,
So strongly shaken
In the grip of the senses:
Gross and grown hard
With stubborn desire
For what is worldly.
How shall he tame it?
Truly, I think
The wind is no wilder.

Sri Krishna: Yes, Arjuna, the mind is restless, no doubt, and hard to subdue. But it can be brought under control by constant practice, and by the exercise of dispassion. Certainly, if a man has no control over his ego, he will find this yoga difficult to master. But a self-controlled man can master it, if he struggles hard, and uses the right means.

Arjuna: Suppose a man has faith, but does not struggle hard enough? His mind wanders away from the practice of yoga and he fails to reach perfection. What will become of him then?

When a man goes astray from the path to Brahman, he has missed both lives, the wordly and the spiritual. He has no support anywhere. Is he not lost, as a broken cloud is lost in the sky?

This is the doubt that troubles me, Krishna; and only you can altogether remove it from my mind. Let me hear your answer.

Sri Krishna: No, my son. That man is not lost, either in this world or the next. No one who seeks Brahman ever comes to an evil end.

Even if a man falls away from the practice of yoga, he will still win the heaven of the doers of good deeds, and dwell there many long years. After that, he will be reborn in the home of pure and prosperous parents. He may even be born into a family of illumined yogis. But such a birth in this world is more difficult to obtain.

He will then regain that spiritual discernment which he acquired in his former body; and so he will strive harder than ever for perfection. Because of his practices in the previous life, he will be driven on toward union with Brahman even in spite of himself. For the man who has once asked the way to Brahman goes further than any mere fulfiller of the

Vedic rituals. By struggling hard, and cleansing himself of all impurities, that yogi will move gradually toward perfection through many births, and reach the highest goal at last.

Great is that yogi who seeks to be
with Brahman.
Greater than those who mortify
the body.
Greater than the learned,
Greater than the doers of good works;
Therefore, Arjuna become a yogi.

He gives me all his heart,
He worships me in faith and love,
That yogi, above every other
I call my very own.

CHAPTER VII

Knowledge And Experience

Sri Krishna: Devote your whole mind to me and practise yoga. Take me for your only refuge. I will tell you how, by doing this, you can know me in my total reality, without any shadow of doubt. I will give you all this knowledge, and direct spiritual experience, besides When a man has that, nothing else in this world remains to be known.

Who cares to seek
For that perfect freedom?
One man, perhaps,
In many thousands.

Then tell me how many
Of those who seek freedom
Shall know the total
Truth of my being?
Perhaps one only.

My Prakriti is of eightfold composition: earth, water, fire, air, ether, mind, intellect and ego.[1] You must understand that behind this, and distinct from it, is that which is the principle of consciousness in all beings, and the source of life in all. It sustains the universe.

Know this my Prakriti
United with me:
The womb of all beings.

---

1. See Appendix.

I am the birth of this cosmos:
Its dissolution also.

I am he who causes:
No other besides me.
Upon me, these worlds are held
Like pearls strung on a thread.

I am the essence of the waters,
The shining of the sun and the moon;
OM in all the Vedas,
The word that is God.
It is I who resound in the ether
And am potent in man.

I am the sacred smell of the earth,
The light of the fire,
Life of all lives,
Austerity of ascetics.

Know me, eternal seed
Of everything that grows:

The intelligence of those who
understand,
The vigour of the active.
In the strong, I am strength
Unhindered by lust
And the objects of craving;
I am all that a man may desire
Without transgressing
The law of his nature.

You must know that whatever belongs to the states of sattwa, rajas and tamas, proceeds from me. They are contained in me, but I am not in them. The entire world is deluded by the moods and mental states which are the expression of these three gunas. That is why the world fails to recognize me as I really am. I stand apart from them all, supreme and deathless.

How hard to break through
Is this, my Maya,
Made of the gunas!
But he who takes refuge
Within me only
Shall pass beyond Maya:
He, and no other.

The evil-doers
Turn not toward me:
These are deluded.
Sunk low among mortals.

Their judgment is lost
In the maze of Maya,
Until the heart
Is human no longer:

Changed within
To the heart of a devil.

Among those who are purified by their good deeds, there are four kinds of men who worship me: the world-weary, the seeker for knowledge, the seeker for happiness and the man of spiritual discrimination. The man of discrimination is the highest of these. He is continually united with me. He devotes himself to me always, and to no other. For I am very dear to that man, and he is dear to me.

Certainly, all these are noble:
But the man of discrimination
I see as my very Self.
For he alone loves me

Because I am myself:
The last and only goal
Of his devoted heart.

Through many a long life
His discrimination ripens:
He makes me his refuge,
Knows that Brahman is all.
How rare are such great ones!

Men whose discrimination has been blunted by wordly desires, establish this or that ritual or cult and resort to various deities, according to the impulse of their inborn natures. But it does not matter what deity a devotee chooses to worship. If he has faith, I make his faith unwavering. Endowed with the faith I give him, he worships that deity, and gets from it everything he prays for. In reality, I alone am the giver.

But these men of small understanding only pray for what is transient and perishable. The worshippers of the devas will go to the devas. So, also, my devotees will come to me.

Thus think the ignorant: that I,
the unmanifest,
Am become man. They do not
know my nature
That is one with Brahman,
changeless, superhuman,
Veiled in my Maya, I am not shown
to many.

How shall this world, bewildered
by delusion,
Recognize me, who am not born
and change not?

I know all beings, Arjuna: past, present and to come. But no one knows me.

All living creatures are led astray as soon as they are born, by the delusion, that this relative world is real. This delusion arises from their own desire and hatred. But the doers of good deeds, whose bad karma is exhausted, are freed from this delusion about the relative world. They hold firmly to their vows, and worship me.

Men take refuge in me, to escape from their fear of old age and death. Thus they come to know Brahman, and the entire nature of the Atman, and the creative energy which is in Brahman. Knowing me, they understand the nature of the relative world and the individual man, and of God who presides over all action. Even at the hour of death, they continue to know me thus. In that hour, their whole consciousness is made one with mine.

CHAPTER VIII

The Way To Eternal Brahman

Arjuna: Tell me, Krishna, what Brahman is. What is the Atman, and what is the creative energy of Brahman? Explain the nature of this relative world, and of the individual man.

Who is God who presides over action in this body, and how does He dwell here? How are you revealed at the hour of death to those whose consciousness is united with you?

Sri Krishna: Brahman is that which is immutable, and independent of any cause but itself. When we consider Brahman as lodged within the individual being, we call Him the Atman. The creative energy of Brahman is that which causes all existences to come into being.

The nature of the relative world is mutability. The nature of the individual man is his consciousness of ego. I alone am God who presides over action, here in this body.

At the hour of death, when a man leaves his body, he must depart with his consciousness absorbed in me. Then he will be united with me. Be certain of that. Whatever a man remembers at the last, when he is leaving the body, will be realized by him in the hereafter; because that will be what his mind has most constantly dwelt on, during this life.

Therefore you must remember me at all times, and do your duty. If your mind and heart are set upon me constantly, you will come to me. Never doubt this.

Make a habit of practising meditation, and do not let your mind be distracted. In this way you will come finally to the Lord who is the light-giver, the highest of the high.

He is all-knowing God, lord of
the emperors,

Ageless, subtler far than mind's
inmost subtlety,
Universal sustainer,
Shining sunlike, self-luminous.

What fashion His form has, who
shall conceive of it?
He dwells beyond delusion,
the dark of Maya.
On Him let man meditate
Always, for then at the last hour

Of going hence from his body,
he will be strong
In the strength of this yoga,
faithfully followed:
The mind is firm, and the heart
So full, it hardly holds its love.

Thus he will take his leave: and
now, with the life-force

Indrawn utterly, held fast between
the eyebrows
He goes forth to find his Lord.
That light-giver, who is greatest.

Now I will tell you briefly about the nature of Him who is called the deathless by those seers who truly understand the Vedas. Devotees enter into Him when the bonds of their desire are broken. To reach this goal, they practise control of the passions.

When a man leaves his body and departs,[1] he must close all the doors

---

1. According to yoga technique, the yogi must employ a special method of leaving the body at death. First, the vital

of the senses. Let him hold the mind firmly within the shrine of the heart, and fix the life-force between the eyebrows. Then let him take refuge in steady concentration, uttering the sacred syllable OM and meditating upon me. Such a man reaches the highest goal. When a yogi has meditated upon me unceasingly for many years, with an undistracted mind, I am easy of access to him, because he is always absorbed in me.

---

force is drawn up the sushumna, the central and spinal passage, and gathered in the brain, "between the eyebrows." The yogi then leaves the body through an aperture in the centre of the brain, called the sahasrara.

Great souls who find me have found the highest perfection. They are no longer reborn into this condition of transience and pain.

All the worlds, and even the heavenly realm of Brahma,[1] are subject to the laws of rebirth. But, for the man who comes to me, there is no returning.

---

1. Brahma (not to be confused with Brahman) is God in the aspect of creator—one of the Hindu Trinity, with Vishnu, the preserver, and Shiva the dissolver. Also see Appendix.

According to Hindu mythology, the words are variously classified as three, seven or fourteen. The Brahma-loka, (realm of Brahma) is said to be the highest.

There is day also, and night in the universe:
The wise know this, declaring the day of Brahma
A thousand ages in span
And the night a thousand ages.[1]
Day dawns, and all those lives that lay hidden asleep
Come forth and show themselves, mortally manifest:
Night falls, and all are dissolved
Into the sleeping germs of life.
Thus they are seen, O Prince, and appear unceasingly,
Dissolving with the dark, and with day returning.
Back to the new birth, new death:
All helpless. They do what they must.

---

1. See Appendix.

But behind the manifest and the unmanifest, there is another Existence which is eternal and changeless. This is not dissolved in the general cosmic dissolution. It has been called the unmanifest, the imperishable. To reach It is said to be the greatest of all achievements. It is my highest state of being. Those who reach It are not reborn. That highest state of being, can only be achieved through devotion to Him in whom all creatures exist, and by whom this universe is pervaded.

I show you two paths.[1]

---

1. The "path of no return" is called in the Upanishads the Deva-Yana, "the path

Let a yogi choose either
When he leaves this body:
The path that leads back to birth,
The path of no return.
There is the path of light,

Of fire and day,
The path of the moon's bright fortnight
And the six months' journey
Of the sun to the north:

---

of the bright ones," who are liberated from rebirth. The path that leads back to birth is the Pitri-Yana, "the path of the fathers," who reach the "lunar light" (a paradise subject to the laws of time) and must ultimately be reborn.

Fire, light, smoke, night, etc., probably represent stages of the soul's experience after death. Thus, light may symbolize knowledge; and smoke ignorance.

The knower of Brahman
Who takes this path
Goes to Brahman:
He does not return.
There is the path of night and smoke,
The path of the moon's dark fortnight
And the six months' journey
Of the sun to the south:
The yogi who takes this path
Will reach the lunar light:
This path leads back
To human birth, at last.

These two paths, the bright and the dark, may be said to have existed in this world of change from a time without any beginning. By the one, a man goes to the place of no return. By the other, he comes back to human birth. No yogi who knows these two paths is ever misled. Therefore, Arjuna, you must be steadfast in yoga, always.

The scriptures declare that merit can be acquired by studying the Vedas, performing ritualistic sacrifices, practising austerities and giving alms. But the yogi who has understood this teaching of mine will gain more than any who do these things. He will reach that universal source, which is the uttermost abode of God.

Chapter IX

The Yoga Of Mysticism

Sri Krishna:

Since you accept me
And do not question,
Now I shall tell you
That innermost secret:
Knowledge of God
Which is nearer than knowing.
Open vision

Direct and instant,
Understand this
And be free forever
From birth and dying
With all their evil.

This is the knowledge
Above all other: purifier
And king of secrets,
Only made plain
To the eye of the mystic.
Great is its virtue,
Its practice easy:
Thus man is brought
To truth eternal.

Those without faith
In this, my knowledge,
Shall fail to find me:
Back they must turn
To the mortal pathway,
Subject still
To birth and to dying.

This entire universe is pervaded by me in that eternal form of mine which is not manifest to the senses. Although I am not within any creature, all creatures exist within me. I do not mean that they exist within me physically. That is my divine mystery. You must try to understand its nature. My Being sustains all creatures and brings them to birth but has no physical contact with them.

For, as the vast air, wandering worldwide
Remains within the ether always,
So they, my wandering creatures,
Are always within me.

These, when the round of ages is accomplished.
I gather back to the seed of their becoming:

These I send forth again
At the hour of creation.[1]

Helpless all, for Maya is their master,
And I, their Lord, the master of this Maya:
Ever and again, I send these multitudes
Forth from my Being.

How shall these acts bind me, who am
Indifferent
To the fruit they bear? For my spirit
Stands apart, watching over
Maya, the maker.

Maya makes all things: what moves,
what is unmoving.
O son of Kunti, that is why the world
spins,
Turning its wheel through birth
And through destruction.

---

1. See Appendix.

Fools pass blindly by the place of my
dwelling
Here in the human form, and of my
majesty
They know nothing at all,
Who am the Lord, their soul.

Vain is their hope, and in vain their
labour, their knowledge:
All their understanding is but
bewilderment:
Their nature has fallen into the madness
Of the friends and monsters.

Great in soul are they who become
what is godlike:
They alone know me, the origin, the
deathless:
They offer me the homage
Of an unwavering mind.

Praising my might with heart and lips
forever,
Striving for the virtue that wins me
and steadfast
In all their vows, they worship adoring,
One with me always.

Others worship me knowing Brahman
in all things:
Some see me one with themselves, or
separate:
Some bow to the countless gods that
are only
My million faces.

Rites that the Vedas ordain, and the
rituals taught by the scriptures:
All these am I, and the offering made
to the ghosts of the fathers,

Herbs of healing and food, the
mantram,[1] the clarified butter:
I the oblation, and I the flame into
which it is offered.

I am the sire of the world, and this
world's mother and grandsire:
I am He who awards to each the fruit
of his action:
I make all things clean, I am OM,
I am absolute knowledge:
I am also the Vedas—the Sama,
the Rig and the Yajus.
I am the end of the path, the witness,
the Lord, the sustainer:

1. Name, or names, of God, which the devotee must repeat and meditate upon. An individual mantram is given by the teacher to each of his disciples at the time of initiation.

I am the place of abode, the beginning,
the friend and the refuge:
I am the breaking-apart and the
storehouse of life's dissolution:
I lie under the seen, of all creatures
the seed that is changeless.
I am the heat of the sun; and the heat
of the fire am I also;
Life eternal and death. I let loose
the rain, or withhold it.
Arjuna, I am the cosmos revealed, and
its germ that lies hidden.

They that are versed
In the triple Veda,
Worshipping me
With the rites appointed,
Drinking the wine
Of the gods communion,

Cleansed from their sinning:
These men pray
For passage to heaven.

Thus attaining
The realm of Indra,
Home of the happy;
There they delight
In celestial pleasures.
Pleasures more spacious
Than any earthly
They taste awhile,
Till the merit that won them
Is all exhausted:
Then they return
To the world of mortals.

Thus go the righteous
Who follow the road
Of the triple Veda

In formal observance:
Hungry still
For the food of the senses,
Drawn by desire
To endless returning.

But if a man will worship me, and meditate upon me with an undistracted mind, devoting every moment to me, I shall supply all his needs, and protect his possessions from loss. Even those whc worship other deities, and sacrifice to them with faith in their hearts, are really worshipping me, though with a mistaken approach. For I am the only enjoyer and the only God of all sacrifices. Nevertheless, such men must return to life on earth, because they do not recognize me in my true nature.

Those who sacrifice to the various deities, will go to those deities. The ancestor-worshippers will go to their ancestors. Those who worship elemental powers and spirits will go to them. So, also, my devotees will come to me.

Whatever man gives me
In true devotion:
Fruit or water.
A leaf, a flower:
I will accept it.
The gift is love.
His heart's dedication.

Whatever your action,
Food or worship;
That you give to another;
Whatever the gift,
Whatever you vow
To the work of the spirit:
O son of Kunti,
Lay these also
As offerings before me.

Thus you will free yourself from both the good and the evil effects of your actions. Offer up everything to me. If your heart is united with me, you will be set free from karma even in this life, and come to me at the last.

My face is equal
To all creation,
Loving no one

Nor hating any.
Nevertheless,
My devotees dwell
Within me always:
I also show forth
And am seen within them.

Though a man be soiled
With the sins of a lifetime,
Let him but love me,
Rightly resolved,
In utter devotion:
I see no sinner,
That man is holy.

Holiness soon
Shall refashion his nature
To peace eternal;
O son of Kunti,
Of this be certain:

The man that loves me,
He shall not perish.

Even those who belong to the lower castes—women. Vaishyas,[1] and Sudras too—can reach the highest spiritual realization, if they will take refuge in me. Need I tell you, then, that this is also true of the holy Brahmins and pious philosopher-kings?

---

1. The four Hindu castes are; Brahmins (the priests), Kshatrivas (the warriors), Vaishyas (the merchants) and Sudras (the servants). Compare, Chapter XVIII, page 219, where the caste-names are used with a more psychological significance and have been translated accordingly.

You find yourself in this transient, joyless world. Turn from it, and take your delight in me. Fill your heart and mind with me, adore me, make all your acts an offering to me, bow down to me in self-surrender. If you set your heart upon me thus, and take me for your ideal above all others, you will come into my Being.

CHAPTER X

Divine Glory

Sri Krishna:

Once more, warrior,
Hear this highest
Word of my wisdom:
Wishing your welfare,
To you I teach it
Since your heart
Delights in the telling.

How shall the mighty
Seers or the devas
Know my beginning?
I am the origin,
I the sustainer
Of seers and devas.

Who knows me birthless,
Never-beginning,
Lord of the worlds:
He alone among mortals
Is stainless of sin,
Unvexed by delusion.

All that makes Man
In his many natures:
Knowledge and power
Of understanding
Unclouded by error.
Truth, forbearance
Calm of spirit.

Control of senses,
Happiness, sorrow,
Birth and destruction;
What fears, what is fearless,
What harms no creature,
The mind unshaken,

The heart contented,
The will austere.
The hand of the giver,
Fame, honour,
And infamy also:
It is by me only
That these are allotted.

Forth from my thought
Came the seven Sages
The Ancient Four
And at last the Manus:
Thus I gave birth
To the first begetters
Of all earth's children.

Who truly knows me,
In manifold Being
Everywhere present
And all-prevailing,

Dwells in my yoga
That shall not be shaken:
Of this be certain.

I am where all things began, the
issuing-forth of the creatures,
Known to the wise in their love when
they worship with hearts overflowing;

Mind and sense are absorbed, I alone
am the theme of their discourse:
Thus delighting each other, they live in
bliss and contentment.

Always aware of their Lord are they,
and ever-devoted:
Therefore the strength of their thought
is illumined and guided towards me.

There in the ignorant heart' where I
dwell, by the grace of my mercy.

I am knowledge, that brilliant lamp,
dispelling its darkness.

Arjuna:

You are Brahman, the highest abode,
the utterly holy:
All the sages proclaim you eternal,
Lord of the devas.
Saintly Narada knew you the birthless,
the everywhere-present:
Devala echoed your praise; Asita too
and Vyasa[1]*:*
Now I also have heard, for to me your
own lips have confirmed it,
Krishna, this is the truth that you tell.
My heart bids me believe you.
God of gods, Lord of the world, Life's
Source, O King of all creatures:

1. Ancient sages.

How shall deva or titan know all the
extent of your glory?
You alone know what you are, by the
light of your innermost nature.
Therefore teach me now, and hold
back no word in the telling,
All the sum of your shapes by which
the three worlds are pervaded;
Tell me how you will make yourself
known to my meditation;
Show me beneath what form and
disguise I must learn to behold you;
Number them all, your heavenly
powers, your manifestations:
Speak, for each word is immortal
nectar: I never grow weary.

Sri Krishna: O Arjuna, I will indeed make known to you my

divine manifestations: but I shall name the chief of these only. For, of the lesser variations in all their detail, there is no end.

I am the Atman that dwells in the in the heart of every mortal creature: I am the beginning, the life-span, and the end of all.

I am Vishnu: I am the radiant sun among the light-givers: I am Marichi, the wind-god: among the stars of night, I am the moon.

I am the Sama Veda: I am Indra, king of heaven: of sense-organs, I am the mind: I am consciousness in the living.

I am Shiva: I am the Lord of all riches: I am the spirit of fire: I am Meru among the mountain peaks.

Know me as Brihaspati, leader of the high priests, and as Skanda, the warrior-chief: I am the ocean among the waters.

I am Bhrigu, the great seer: among words, I am the sacred syllable OM: I am the vow of japam[1]; I am Himalaya among the things that cannot be moved.

I am the holy fig tree: I am Narada, the godly sage, Chitraratha,

---

1. The practice of repeating a mantram (name of God). See note on Chapter IX. page 172.

the celestial musician, and Kapila among the perfected souls.

Among horses, you may know me as Uchcaishravas who was brought forth from the sea of nectar: I am Airavata among royal elephants: I am king among men.

Of weapons, I am God's thunderbolt: I am Kamadhenu, the heavenly cow: I am the love-god, begetter of children: I am Vasuki, god of snakes.

I am Ananta, the holy serpent: of water-beings, I am Varuna: Aryaman among the Fathers: I am Death, who distributes the fruit of all action.

I am Prahlada, the giant: among those who measure, I am Time: I am the lion among beasts: Vishnu's eagle among the birds.

Among purifiers, I am the wind: I am Rama among the warriors: the shark among fish: Ganges among the rivers.

I am the beginning, the middle and the end in creation: I am the knowledge of things spiritual: I am the logic of those who debate.

In the alphabet, I am A: among compounds, the copulative: I am Time without end: I am the Sustainer: my face is everywhere.

I am death that snatches all; I, also am the source of all that shall be born; I am glory, prosperity, beautiful speech: memory, intelligence, steadfastness and forgiveness.

I am the great Sama of the Vedic hymns, and the Gayatri among poetic metres; of the months. I am Marga-shirsha[1]: of seasons, the time of flowers.

I am the dice-play of the cunning: I am the strength of the strong: I am

---

1. A month of the Hindu year, including parts of November and December.

triumph and perseverance: I am the Sattwa[1] of the good.

I am Krishna among the Vrishnis, Arjuna among the Pandavas, Vyasa among the sages. Ushanas among the illumined poets.

I am the sceptre and the mastery of those who rule, the policy of those who seek to conquer: I am the silence of things secret; I am the knowledge of the knower.

O Arjuna, I am the divine seed of all lives. In this world, nothing animate or inanimate exists without me.

1. See Appendix.

There is no limit to my divine manifestations, nor can they be numbered, O foe-consumer. What I have described to you are only a few of my countless forms.

Whatever in this world is powerful, beautiful or glorious, that you may know to have come forth from a fraction of my power and glory.

But what need have you, Arjuna, to know this huge variety? Know only that I exist, and that one atom of myself sustains the universe.

CHAPTER XI

The Vision Of God In His Universal Form

Arjuna: By your grace, you have taught me the truth about the Atman. Your words are mystic and sublime. They have dispelled my ignorance.

From you, whose eyes are like the lotus-flowers, I have learnt in detail of the origin and dissolution of creatures, and of your own infinite glory.

O Supreme Lord, you are as you describe yourself to be: I do not doubt that. Nevertheless I long to behold your divine Form.

If you find me worthy of that vision, then reveal to me, O Master of yogis, your changeless Atman.

Sri Krishna: Behold, O Prince, my divine forms, hundreds upon thousands, various in kind, various in colour and in shape.

Behold the Adityas, and the Vasus, and the Rudras, and the Aswins, and the Maruts[1]. Behold many wonders, O descendant of Bharata, that no man has seen before.

O conqueror of sloth, this very day you shall behold the whole universe with all things animate and

---

1. Various classes of celestial beings.

inert made one within this body of mine. And whatever else you desire to see, that you shall see also.

But you cannot see me thus with those human eyes. Therefore, I give you divine sight. Behold—this is my yoga power.

Sanjaya: Then, O King, when he had spoken these words, Sri Krishna, Master of all yogis, revealed to Arjuna his transcendent, divine Form, speaking from innumerable mouths, seeing with a myriad eyes, of many marvellous aspects, adorned with countless divine ornaments, brandishing all kinds of heavenly weapons, wearing celestial garlands and the raiment of paradise, anointed with perfumes of heavenly fragrance, full of revelations, resplendent, boundless, of ubiquitous regard.

Suppose a thousand suns should rise together into the sky: such is the glory of the Shape of Infinite God.

Then the son of Pandu beheld the entire universe, in all its multitudinous diversity, lodged as one being within the body of the God of gods.

Then was Arjuna, that lord of mighty riches, overcome with wonder. His hair stood erect. He bowed low before God in adoration, and clasped his hands, and spoke:

Arjuna:

Ah, my God, I see all gods within
your body;
Each in his degree, the multitude of
creatures;
See Lord Brahma throned upon the
lotus;
See all the sages, and the holy serpents.

Universal Form, I see you without limit.
Infinite of arms, eyes, mouths and
bellies—
See, and find no end midst, or beginning.
Crowned with diadems, you wield the
mace and discus.

Shining every way—the eyes shrink
from your splendour
Brilliant like the sun; like fire, blazing,
boundless.

You are all we know, supreme,
beyond man's measure,
This world's sure-set plinth and
refuge never shaken.
Guardian of eternal law, life's Soul
undying.

Birthless, deathless; yours the
strength titanic,
Million-armed, the sun and moon your
eyeballs,
Fiery-faced, you blast the world to
ashes,

Fill the sky's four corners., span the
chasm
Sundering heaven from each. Superb
and awful
Is your Form that makes the three
worlds tremble.

Into you, the companies of devas
Enter with clasped hands, in dread
and wonder.
Crying "Peace", the Rishis and the
Siddhas
Sing your praise with hymns of
adoration.

Adityas and Rudras, Sadhyas, Viswas,
Aswins,
Maruts and Vasus, the hosts of the
Gandharvas,
Yakshas, Asuras, Ushmapas and
Siddhas—
All of them gaze upon you in
amazement.

At the sight of this, your Shape
stupendous,
Full of mouths and eyes, feet, thighs
and bellies.

Terrible with fangs, O mighty master,
All the worlds are fear-struck, even as
I am.

When I see you, Vishnu, omnipresent,
Shouldering the sky in hues of rainbow,
With your mouths agape and flame-
eyes staring—
All my peace is gone; my heart is
troubled.

Now with frightful tusks your mouths
are gnashing.
Flaring like the fires of Doomsday
morning—
North, south, east and west seem all
confounded—
Lord of devas, world's abode, have
mercy!

Dhritarashtra's offspring, many a
monarch,

Bhishma, Drona, and the son of Suta,
There they go—with our warriors also—
Hurrying to your jaws, wide-fanged and hideous—
See where mangled heads lie crushed between them!

Swift as many rivers streaming to the ocean,
Rush the heroes to your fiery gullets:
Mothlike, to meet the flame of their destruction,
Headlong these plunge into you, and perish.
Licking with your burning tongues, devouring
All the worlds you probe the heights of heaven
With intolerable beams O Vishnu.

Tell me who you are, and were from the beginning.
You of aspect grim. O God of gods, be gracious.
Take my homage, Lord. From me your ways are hidden.

Sri Krishna:

I am come as Time the waster of the peoples,
Ready for that hour that ripens to their ruin.
All these hosts must die; strike stay your hand—no matter.
Therefore; strike. Win kingdom, wealth and glory.
Arjuna arise, O ambidextrous bowman.

Seem to slay. By me these men are slain already.

You but smite the dead, the doom-
devoted heroes.
Jayadratha, Drona, Bhishma, Karna.
Fight, and have no fear. The foe is
yours to conquer.

Sanjaya: After Arjuna had heard these words of the Lord Krishna, he folded his palms and bowed down, trembling. Prostrating himself, with great fear, he addressed Krishna once more, in a choking voice:

Arjuna:

Well it is the world delights to do
you honour!
At the sight of you, O master of the
senses,
Demons scatter every way in terror,

And the hosts of Siddhas bow adoring.
Mightiest, how should they indeed
withhold their homage?
O Prime Cause of all, even Brahma
the Beginner—
Deathless, world's abode, and Lord
of devas,
You are what is not, what is, and
what transcends them.

You are first and highest in heaven,
O ancient Spirit.
It is within you the cosmos rests in
safety.
You are known and knower, goal of
all our striving.
Endless in your change, your body
forth creation.

Lord of fire and death, of wind and
moon and waters,

Father of the born, and this world's
Father's Father.
Hail, all hail to you—a thousand
salutations.

Take our salutations, Lord, from
every quarter.
Infinite of might and boundless in
your glory
You are all that is, since everywhere
we find you.

Carelessly I called you "Krishna" and
"my comrade,"
Took undying God for friend and
fellow-mortal,
Overbold with love, unconscious of
your greatness.

Often I would jest, familiar, as we
feasted

Midst the throng, or walked, or lay
at rest together:
Did my words offend? Forgive me,
Lord Eternal.
Author of this world, the unmoved
and the moving,
You alone are fit for worship, you
the highest.
Where in the three worlds shall any
find your equal?
Therefore I bow down prostrate and
ask for pardon:
Now forgive me, God, as friend
forgives his comrade,
Father forgives son, and man his
dearest lover.

I have seen what no man ever saw
before me;
Deep is my delight, but still
my dread is greater.

Show me now your other Form,
O Lord, be gracious.
Thousand-membered, Universal
Being,
Show me now the Shape I knew of
old, the four-armed,[1]
With your diadem and mace,
the discus-bearer.

---

1. The only explanation of this passage seems to be that Arjuna is asking Sri Krishna to assume the shape of his chosen deity, Vishnu—since it cannot mean that Krishna had four arms while in his human shape. If this interpretation is correct, we may assume that God took in the four-armed shape of Vishnu for a moment, before reappearing as Krishna. As has been stated elsewhere, Krishna was regarded as an incarnation of Vishnu.

Sri Krishna:

This my Form of fire, world-wide,
supreme, primeval,
Manifest by yoga power, alone of all men,
Arjuna, I showed to you because
I love you.
Neither through sacrifice nor study of
the Vedas,
Nor strict austerities, nor alms, nor
rituals,
Shall this my Shape be viewed by any
mortal,
Other than you, O hero of the Pandus.

Now you need fear no more, nor be
bewildered,
Seeing me so terrible. Be glad, take
courage.
Look, here am I, transformed, as first
you knew me.

Sanjaya: Having spoken thus to Arjuna, Krishna appeared in his own Shape. The Great-Souled One, assuming once more his mild and pleasing form, brought peace to him in his terror.

Arjuna: O Krishna, now that I see your pleasant human form, I am myself again.

Sri Krishna: That Shape of mine which you have seen is very difficult to behold. Even the devas themselves are always longing to see it. Neither by study of the Vedas, nor by austerities, nor by almsgiving, nor by rituals can I be seen as you have seen me. But by single-minded and intense devotion, that Form of mine may be completely known, and seen and entered into, O consumer of the foe.

Whosoever works for me alone, makes me his only goal and is devoted to me, free from attachment, and without hatred towards any creature—that man, O Prince, shall enter into me.

Chapter XII

The Yoga Of Devotion

Arjuna: Some worship you with steadfast love. Others worship God the unmanifest and changeless. Which kind of devotee has the greater understanding of yoga?

Sri Krishna: Those whose minds are fixed on me in steadfast love, worshipping me with absolute faith, I consider them to have the greater understanding of yoga.

As for those others, the devotees of God the unmanifest indefinable and changeless, they worship that which is omnipresent, constant, eternal, beyond thought's compass, never to be moved. They hold all the senses in check. They are tranquil-minded, and devoted to the welfare of humanity. They see the Atman in every creature. They also will certainly come to me.

But the devotees of the unmanifest have a harder task, because the unmanifest is very difficult for embodied souls to realize.

Quickly I come
To those who offer me
Every action,
Worship me only.

Their dearest delight,
With devotion undaunted.

Because they love me
These are my bondsmen
And I shall save them
From mortal sorrow
And all the waves
Of Life's deathly ocean.

Be absorbed in me,
Lodge your mind in me:
Thus you shall dwell in me,
Do not doubt it,
Here and hereafter.

If you cannot become absorbed in me, then try to reach me by repeated concentration. If you lack the strength to concentrate, then devote yourself to works which will please me. For, by working for my sake only, you will achieve perfection. If you cannot even do this, then surrender yourself to me altogether. Control the lusts of your heart, and renounce the fruits of every action.

Concentration which is practised with discernment is certainly better than the mechanical repetition of a ritual or a prayer. Absorption in God—to live with Him and be one with Him always—is even better than concentration. But renunciation brings instant peace to the spirit.

A man should not hate any living-creature. Let him be friendly and compassionate to all. He must free himself from the delusion of "I" and "mine". He must accept pleasure and pain with an equal tranquillity. He must be forgiving, ever-contented, self-controlled, united constantly with me in his meditation. His resolve must be unshakable. He must be dedicated to me in intellect and in mind. Such a devotee is dear to me.

He neither molests his fellowmen, nor allows himself to become disturbed by the world. He is no longer swayed by joy and envy, anxiety and fear. Therefore he is dear to me.

He is pure, and independent of the body's desire. He is able to deal with the unexpected; prepared for everything, unperturbed by anything. He is neither vain nor anxious about the results of his actions. Such a devotee is dear to me.

He does not desire or rejoice in what is pleasant. He does not dread what is unpleasant, or grieve over it. He remains unmoved by good or evil fortune. Such a devotee is dear to me.

His attitude is the same toward friend and foe. He is indifferent to honour and insult, heat and cold, pleasure and pain. He is free from attachment. He values praise and blame equally. He can control his speech. He is content with whatever he gets. His home is everywhere and nowhere. His mind is fixed upon me, and his hearts is full of devotion. He is dear to me.

This true wisdom I have taught will lead you to immortality. The faithful practise it with devotion, taking me for their highest aim. To me they surrender heart and mind. They are exceedingly dear to me.

CHAPTER XIII

The Field And Its Knower

Arjuna: And now, Krishna, I wish to learn about Prakriti and Brahman, the Field and the Knower of the Field. What is knowledge? What is it that has to be known?

Sri Krishna.: This body is called the Field because a man sows seeds of action in it and reaps their fruits. Wise men say that the Knower of the Field is he who watches what takes place within this body.

Recognize me as the Knower of the Field in every body. I regard discrimination between Field and Knower as the highest kind of knowledge.

Now listen and I will tell you briefly what the Field is; its nature modifications and origin. I will tell you also who the Knower is and what are his powers.

The sages have expressed these truths variously in many hymns and in aphorisms on the nature of Brahman, subtly reasoned and convincing in their arguments.

Briefly I name them:

First. Prakriti
Which is the cosmos
In cause unseen

And visible feature;
Intellect, ego;
Earth, water and ether,
Air and fire;
Man's ten organs
Of knowing, and doing,
Man's mind also:
The five sense-objects[1]
Sound in its essence.
Essence of aspect,
Essence of odour,
Of touch and tasting;
Hate and desire,
And pain and pleasure;
Consciousness, lastly,
And resolution;
These, with their sum
Which is blent in the body;

1. See Appendix.

These make the Field
With its limits and changes.

Therefore I tell you:
Be humble, be harmless.
Have no pretension.
Be upright, forbearing,
Serve your teacher
In true obedience,
Keeping the mind
And the body in cleanness.
Tranquil, steadfast,
Master of ego,
Standing apart
From the things of the senses,
Free from self;
Aware of the weakness
In mortal nature,
Its bondage to birth,
Age, suffering, dying;
To nothing be slave,

Nor desire possession
Of man, child or wife.
Of home or of household:
Calmly encounter
The painful, the pleasant;
Adore me only
With heart undistracted;
Turn all your thought
Toward solitude, spurning
The noise of the crowd,
Its fruitless commotion;
Strive without ceasing
To know the Atman.
Seek this knowledge
And comprehend clearly
Why you should seek it:
Such, it is said,
Are the roots of true wisdom:
Ignorance, merely,
Is all that denies them.

Now I shall describe. That which has to be known, in order that its knower may gain immortality. That Brahman is beginningless, transcendent, eternal. He is said to be equally beyond what is, and what is not.

Everywhere are His hands, eyes, feet;
His heads and His faces:
This whole world is His ear; He exists,
encompassing all things;
Doing the tasks of each sense. Yet
Himself devoid of the senses:
Standing apart, He sustains: He is
free from the gunas but feels them.
He is within and without: He lives in
the live and the lifeless:
Subtle beyond mind's grasp; so near
us, so utterly distant:

Undivided, He seems to divide into
objects and creatures;
Sending creation forth from Himself,
He upholds and withdraws it:
Light of all lights, He abides, beyond
our ignorant darkness;
Knowledge, the one thing real we may
study or know, the heart's dweller.

Now I have told you briefly what the Field is, what knowledge is, and what is that one Reality which must be known. When my devotee knows these things, he becomes fit to reach union with me.

You must understand that both Prakriti and Brahman are without beginning. All evolution and all the gunas proceed from Prakriti. From Prakriti the evolution of body and senses is said to originate. The sense of individuality in us is said to cause our experience of pleasure and pain. The individual self, which is Brahman mistakenly identified with Prakriti, experiences the gunas which proceed from Prakriti. It is born of pure or impure parents, according to that kind of guna to which it is most attached:

The supreme Brahman in this body is also known as the Witness. It makes all our actions possible, and, as it were sanctions them, experiencing all our experiences. It is the infinite

Being, the supreme Atman. He who has experienced Brahman directly and known it to be other than Prakriti and the gunas, will not be reborn, no matter how he has lived his life.

Some, whose hearts are purified, realize the Atman within themselves through contemplation. Some realize the Atman philosophically, by meditating upon its independence of Prakriti. Others realize it by following the yoga of right action. Others, who do not know these paths, worship God as their teachers have taught them. If these faithfully practise what they have learned, they also will pass beyond death's power.

Know this, O Prince:
Of things created
All are come forth
From the seeming union
Of Field and Knower,
Prakriti with Brahman.

Who sees his Lord
Within every creature,
Deathlessly dwelling
Amidst the mortal:
That man sees truly.

Thus ever aware
Of the Omnipresent
Always about him,
He offers no outrage
To his own Atman,
Hides the face of God
Beneath ego no longer:
Therefore he reaches

That bliss which is highest:
Who sees all action
Ever performed
Alone by Prakriti,
That man sees truly:
The Atman is actless.

Who sees the separate
Lives of all creatures
United in Brahman
Brought forth from Brahman,
Himself finds Brahman.

Not subject to change
Is the infinite Atman,
Without beginning,
Beyond the gunas:
Therefore, O Prince,
Though It dwells in the body,
It acts not, nor feels
The fruits of our action.

For, like the ether,
Pervading all things,
Too subtle for taint,
This Atman also
Inhabits all bodies
But never is tainted.

By the single sun
This whole world is illumined;
By its one Knower
The Field is illumined.

Who thus perceives
With the eye of wisdom
In what manner the Field
Is distinct from its Knower,
How men are made free
From the toils of Prakriti:
His aim is accomplished,
He enters the Highest.

CHAPTER XIV

The Three Gunas

Sri Krishna:

Once more I shall teach you
That uttermost wisdom:
The sages who found it
Were all made perfect,
Escaping the bonds of the body.

In that wisdom they lived,
Made one with my holy nature;
Now they are not reborn
When a new age begins,
Nor have they any part
In its dissolution.

Prakriti, this vast womb,
I quicken into birth
With the seed of all life;
Thence, O son of Bharata,
The many creatures spring.

Many are the forms of the living,
Many the wombs that bear them;
Prakriti, the womb of all wombs
And I the seed-giving Father.

From Prakriti gunas come forth
Sattwa, rajas, tamas:
These are the bonds that bind
The undying dweller
Imprisoned in the body.

Sattwa the shining
Can show the Atman
By its pure light:

Yet sattwa will bind you
To search for happiness,
Longing for knowledge.

Rajas the passionate
Will make you thirsty
For pleasure and possession :
Rajas will bind you
To hunger for action.

Tamas the ignorant
Bewilders all men:
Tamas will bind you
With bonds of delusion,
Sluggishness, stupor.
The power of sattwa
Enslaves the happy,
The power of rajas
Enslaves the doers,
The power of tamas

Enslaves the deluded
And darkens their judgment.

When sattwa prevails
Over rajas, tamas,
Man feels that sattwa:
When rajas prevails
Over sattwa, tamas,
Man is seized by that rajas:
When tamas prevails
Over rajas, sattwa,
Man yields to that tamas.

When understanding
Shines in through the senses,
The door of the body:
Know sattwa is present.
In greed, in the heat of action,
In eager enterprise,

In restlessness, in all desire,
Know rajas the ruler.

When the mind is dark,
Bewildered, slothful
And lost in delusion
Know tamas prevailing.

That man who meets death
In the hour of sattwa
Goes to a sinless home
Among the saints of God.

He who dies in rajas
Will be reborn
Among those whose bondage
is action:
He who dies in tamas will return
To the womb of a dullard.

Fruit of the righteous act
Is sattwa, purest joy:
As for the deeds of rajas,
Pain is their fruit:
Truly, ignorance is all
The fruit of tamas.

Of sattwa, knowledge is born;
Of rajas, greed;
Tamas brings forth bewilderment,
Delusion, darkness.

Abiding in sattwa,
Man goes to higher realms;
Remaining in rajas,
In this world he remains;
Sunk in tamas,
His lowest nature,
He sinks to the underworld.

Let the wise man know
These gunas alone as the doers
Of every action;
Let him learn to know That
Which is beyond them, also;
Thus he will reach my oneness.

When the dweller in the body
Has overcome the gunas
That cause this body,
Then he is made free
From birth and death,
From pain and decay:
He becomes immortal.

A man is said to have transcended the gunas when he does not hate the light of sattwa, or the activity of rajas, or even the delusion of tamas, while these prevail; and yet does not long for them after they have ceased. He is like one who sits unconcerned, and is not disturbed by the gunas. He knows that they are the doers of all action and never loses this power of discrimination. He rests in the inner calm of the Atman, regarding happiness and suffering as one. Gold, mud and stone are of equal value to him. The pleasant and the unpleasant are alike. He has true discernment. He pays no attention to praise or to blame. His behaviour is the same when he is honoured and when he is insulted. When men go to war, he does not regard either side as his enemies or his partisans. He feels no lack of anything; therefore he never initiates any action.

He who worships me with unfaltering love transcends these gunas. He becomes fit to reach union with Brahman.

For I am Brahman
Within this body,
Life immortal
That shall not perish:
I am the Truth
And the joy for ever.

CHAPTER XV

Devotion To The Supreme Spirit

Sri Krishna:

There is a fig tree
In ancient story,
The giant Aswattha,
The everlasting,
Rooted in heaven,
Its branches earthward:
Each of its leaves
Is a song of the Vedas,
And he who knows it
Knows all the Vedas.

Downward and upward
Its branches bending

Are fed by the gunas,
The buds it puts forth
Are the things of the senses,
Roots it has also
Reaching downward
Into this world,
The roots of man's action.

What its form is,
Its end and beginning,
Its very nature,
Can never be known here.

Therefore, a man should contemplate Brahman until he has sharpened the axe of his non-attachment. With this axe, he must cut through the firmly-rooted Aswattha tree. Then he must try to realize that state from which there is no return to future births. Let him take refuge in that Primal Being, from whom all this seeming activity streams forth forever.

When men have thrown off their ignorance, they are free from pride and delusion. They have conquered the evil of worldly attachment. They live in constant union with the Atman. All craving has left them. They are no longer at the mercy of opposing sense-reactions. Thus they reach that state which is beyond all change.

This is my Infinite Being; shall
the sun lend it
Any light—or the moon, or fire?

For it shines
Self-luminous always; and he who attains me
Will never be reborn.

Part of myself is the God within every creature,
Keeps that nature eternal, yet seems to be separate.
Putting on mind and senses five; the garment
Made of Prakriti.
When the Lord puts on a body, or casts it from him,
He enters or departs, taking the mind and senses
Away with him, as the wind steals perfume
Out of the flowers.

Watching over the ear and the eye, and presiding
There behind touch, and taste, and smell, he is also
Within the mind: he enjoys and suffers
The things of the senses.

Dwelling in flesh, or departing, or one with the gunas,
Knowing their moods and motions, he is invisible
Always to the ignorant, but his sages see him
With the eye of wisdom.

Yogis who have gained tranquillity through the practice of spiritual disciplines. behold him in their own consciousness. But those who lack tranquillity and discernment will not find him, even though they may try hard to do so.

The light that lives in the sun,
Lighting all the world,
The light of the moon,
The light that is in fire:
Know that light to be mine.

My energy enters the earth,
Sustaining all that lives:
I become the moon,
Giver of water and sap,
To feed the plants and the trees.

Flame of life in all,
I consume the many foods,
Turning them into strength
That upholds the body.

I am in all hearts.
I give and take away
Knowledge and memory:
I am all that the Vedas tell,
I am the teacher,
The knower of Vedanta.

There are two kinds of personality in this world, the mortal and the immortal. The personality of all creatures is mortal. The personality of God is said to be immortal. It is the same forever. But there is one other than these; the Impersonal Being who is called the supreme Atman. He is the unchanging Lord who pervades and supports the three worlds. And since I, the Atman, transcend the mortal and even the immortal, I am known in this world and in the Vedas as the supreme Reality.

He who is free from delusion, and knows me as the supreme Reality, knows all that can be known. Therefore he adores me with his whole heart.

This is the most sacred of all the truths I have taught you. He who has realized it becomes truly wise. The purpose of his life is fulfilled.

Chapter XVI

Divine And Demoniac Tendencies

Sri Krishna: A man who is born with tendencies towards the Divine, is fearless and pure in heart. He perseveres in that path to union with Brahman, which the scriptures and his teacher have taught him. He is charitable. He can control his passions. He studies the scriptures regularly, and obeys their directions. He practises spiritual disciplines. He is straightforward, truthful, and of an even temper. He harms no one. He renounces the things of this world. He has a tranquil mind and an unmalicious tongue. He is compassionate toward all. He is not greedy. He is gentle and modest. He abstains from useless activity. He has faith in the strength of his higher nature. He can forgive and endure. He is clean in thought and act. He is free from hatred and from pride. Such qualities are his birthright.

When a man is born with demoniac tendencies, his birthright is hypocrisy, arrogance, conceit, anger, cruelty and ignorance.

The birthright of the divine nature leads to liberation. The birthright of the demoniac nature leads to greater bondage. But you need not fear, Arjuna! Your birthright is divine.

In this world there are two kinds of beings: those whose nature tends towards the Divine, and those who have the demoniac tendencies. I have already described the divine nature to you in some detail. Now you shall learn more about the demoniac nature.

Men of demoniac nature know neither what they ought to do nor what they should refrain from doing. There is no truth in them, or purity, or right conduct. They maintain that the scriptures are a lie, and that the universe is not based upon a moral law, but godless, conceived in lust and created by population, without any other cause. Because they believe this in the darkness of their little minds, these degraded cratures do horrible deeds, attempting to destroy the world. They are enemies of mankind.

Their lust can never be appeased. They are arrogant, and vain, and drunk with pride. They run blindly after what is evil. The ends they work for are unclean. They are sure that life has only one purpose: gratification of the senses. And so they are plagued by innumerable cares from which death alone can release them. Anxiety binds them with a hundred chains delivering them over to lust and wrath. They are ceaselessly busy, piling up dishonest gains to satisfy their cravings.

"I wanted this, and today I got it. I want that: I shall get it tomorrow. All these riches are now mine: soon I shall have more. I have killed this enemy. I will kill all the rest. I am a ruler of men. I enjoy the things of this world. I am successful, strong and happy. Who is my equal? I am so wealthy and so nobly born. I will sacrifice to the gods. I will give alms. I will make merry." That is what they say to themselves, in the blindness of their ignorance.

They are addicts of sensual pleasure, made restless by their many desires, and caught in the net of delusion. They fall into the filthy hell of their own evil minds. Conceited, haughty, foolishly proud, and intoxicated by their wealth, they offer sacrifice to God in name only, for outward show, without following the sacred rituals. These malignant creatures are full of egoism, vanity, lust, wrath, and' consciousness of power. They loathe me, and deny my presence both in themselves and in others. They are enemies of all men and of myself; cruel, despicable and vile. I cast them back, again and again, into the wombs of degraded parents, subjecting them to the wheel of birth and death. And so they are constantly reborn, in degradation and delusion. They do not reach me, but sink down to the lowest possible condition of the soul.

Hell has three doors: lust, rage and greed. These lead to man's ruin. Therefore he must avoid them all. He who passes by these three dark doors has achieved his own salvation. He will reach the highest goal at last.

But he who flouts the commandments of the scriptures,

and acts on the impulse of his desires, cannot reach perfection, or happiness, or the highest goal.

Let the scriptures be your guide, therefore, in deciding what you must do, and what you must abstain from. First learn the path of action, as the scriptures teach it. Then act accordingly.

CHAPTER XVII

Three Kinds of Faith

Arjuna: There are men who sacrifice to God with faith in their hearts, although they do not follow the instructions of the scriptures. What is the nature of that faith? Does it belong to sattwa, or to rajas, or to tamas?

Sri Krishna: Faith, among human beings, is of three kinds. It is characterized by sattwa, or by rajas, or by tamas. According to a man's dominant tendencies Now listen. The faith of each individual corresponds to his temperament. A man consists of the faith that is in him. Whatever his faith is, he is.

Men whose temperament is dominated by sattwa, worship God, in His various aspects. Men of rajas worship power and wealth. As for the rest—the men of tamas—they worship the spirits of the dead, and make gods of the ghosts of their ancestors.

You may know those men to be of demoniac nature who mortify the body excessively, in ways not prescribed by the scriptures. They do this because their lust and attachment to sense-objects has filled them with egotism and vanity. In their foolishness, they weaken all their sense-organs, and outrage me, the dweller within the body.

The food which is agreeable to different men is also of three sorts. So, too, are the kinds of sacrifice, austerity and alms giving. Listen; this is how they may be distinguished.

Men of sattwa like foods which increase their vital force, energy, strength and health. Such foods add to the pleasure of physical and mental life. They are juicy, soothing, fresh and agreeable. But men of rajas prefer foods which are violently bitter, sour, salty, hot, pungent, acid and burning. These cause ill-health, and distemper of the mind and body. And men of tamas take a perverse pleasure in foods which are stale, tasteless, rotten and impure. They like to eat the leavings of others.

When men offer sacrifice in accordance with scriptural instructions, and do not desire any advantage for themselves, they are inspired by sattwa. Their hearts are set upon the sacrifice, for its own sake. An inner sense of duty impels them. But you may be sure that the performance of sacrifice for outward show, and in the hope of divine reward, is inspired by rajas. When the givers of the sacrifice are inspired by tamas, they disregard the scriptural instructions: there is no food-offering, no prayer of dedication, no gift to the chief priest and no faith at all.

Reverence for the devas, the seers, the teachers and the sages; straight forwardness, harmlessness; physical cleanliness and sexual purity; these are the virtues whose practice is called austerity of the body. To speak without ever causing pain to another, to be truthful, to say always what is kind and beneficial and to study the scriptures regularly; this practice is called austerity of speech. The practice of serenity, sympathy, meditation upon the Atman, withdrawal of the mind from sense-objects, and integrity of motive, is called austerity of the mind. When men practise this threefold austerity devotedly, with enlightened faith and no desire for reward, it is said to have the nature of sattwa.

Austerity which is practised out of selfish pride, or to gain notoriety, honour and worship, is said to have the nature of rajas, Its effect is not lasting, because it lacks resolution. Austerity is said to have the nature of tamas when it is practised for some foolish purpose, or for the excitement of self-torture, or in order to harm another person.[1]

A gift may be regarded as proceeding from sattwa, when it is given to a deserving person, at a suitable time, and in a fit place; not because of past benefits, or in the hope of a future reward, but simply because the giver knows that it is right for him to give. Whatever is given in the hope of a like return, or with any other selfish motive, or reluctantly, may be known to proceed from rajas. From tamas comes the gift which is given to an unworthy person, at the

1. i.e. "Black Magic."

wrong time and in the wrong place, disdainfully, without regard for the feelings of him who receives it.

OM TAT SAT: these three words designate Brahman, by whom the seers, the Vedas and the sacrificial rites were created in ancient times. Therefore OM is always uttered by the devotees of Brahman, as the scriptures direct, before undertaking any act of sacrifice, alms giving or austerity. TAT, meaning the Absolute, is uttered by seekers after liberation who desire no reward for their deed, when they are about to make sacrifice, or give alms, or practise some austerity. SAT means goodness and existence. It also means an auspicious act. All perseverance in sacrifice, austerity or almsgiving is SAT. All actions dedicated to Brahman are SAT.

If a man performs any act of a sacrifice, or gives any gift, or practises any austerity without directing his faith and will toward Brahman, then what he does is ASAT, unreal. It cannot produce any good result, either in this world, or the next.

CHAPTER XVIII

The Yoga Of Renunciation

Arjuna: I want to learn the truth about renunciation and non-attachment. What is the difference between these two principles?

Sri Krishna: The sages tell us that renunciation means the complete giving up of all actions which are motivated by desire. And they say that non-attachment means abandonment of the fruits of action.

Some philosophers declare that all kinds of action should be given up because action always contains a certain measure of evil. Others say that acts of sacrifice, almsgiving and austerity should not be given up. Now you shall hear the truth of this matter.

Acts of sacrifice, almsgiving and austerity should not be given up: their performance is necessary. For sacrifice, almsgiving and austerity are a means of purification to those who rightly understand them. But even these acts must be performed without attachment or regard for their fruits, such is my final and considered judgment.

Renunciation is said to be of three kinds. If a man, in his ignorance renounces those actions which the scriptures ordain, his renunciations is inspired by tamas. If he abstains from any action merely because it is disagreeable, or because he fears it will cause him bodily pain, his renunciation is inspired by rajas. He will not obtain any spiritual benefit from such renunciation. But when a man performs an action which is sanctioned by the scriptures, and does it for duty's sake only, renouncing all attachment and desire for its fruits, then his renunciation is inspired by sattwa.

When a man is endowed with spiritual discrimination and

illumined by knowledge of the Atman, all his doubts are dispelled. He does not shrink from doing what is disagreeable to him, nor does he long to do what is agreeable. No human being can give up action altogether, but he who gives up the fruits of action is said to be non-attached.

To those who have not yet renounced the ego and its desires, action bears three kinds of fruit—pleasant, unpleasant, and a mixture of both. They will be reaped in due season. But those who have renounced ego and desire will reap no fruit at all, either in this world or in the next.

All our action
Has five partakers:
So say the scriptures
That teach us wisdom
To break the bondage
Earned by our action:
Listen and learn them.

First, this body:
Then ego, the doer;
The organs of sense
And the many motions
Of Life in the body;
Lastly, the devas
In spirit presiding.[1]

1. According to Hindu mythology, each sense organ has a presiding deity.

Whatever the action,
Excellent, evil;
Whether of speech,
Of mind, or of body:
These are its causes.

Falsely he sees,
And with small discernment,
Who sees this Atman
The doer of action:
His mind is not purged
In the work of the spirit.

But he whose mind dwells
Beyond attachment,
Untainted by ego,
No act shall blind him
With any bond :
Though he slays these thousands
He is no slayer.

There are three things which motivate action: knowledge, the knower and that which is known. There are three constituents of action: the instrument, the purpose and the doer. Sankhya.[1] philosophy declares that knowledge, action and doer are of three kinds only, according to the guna which predominates in each. Listen, this is their nature.

There is that knowledge
From sattwa proceeding
Which knows one Being
Deathless in every creature
Entire amidst all division.

---

1. The system of philosophy compiled by Kapila.

The knowledge that is rajas
Knows nothing but difference:
Many souls in many creatures,
All various, each
Apart from his fellow.

The knowledge that is tamas
Knows no reason:
Its sight distorted
Takes the part for the whole,
Misreading Nature.

The act of sacred duty,
Done without attachment,
Not as pleasure desired,
Not as hated compulsion,
By him who has no care
For the fruit of his action:
That act is of sattwa.

The act of weary toil

Done in despite of nature
Under the whip of lust
And the will of the ego:
That act is of rajas.

The act undertaken
In the hour of delusion
Without count of cost,
Squandering strength and treasure,
Heedless of harm to another,
By him who does not question
His power to perform it:
That act is of tamas.

The doer without desire,
Who does not boast of his deed,
Who is ardent, enduring,
Untouched by triumph,
In failure untroubled:
He is a man of sattwa.

The doer with desire,
Hot for the prize of vain glory,
Brutal, greedy and foul,
In triumph too quick to rejoice,
In failure despairing:
He is a man of rajas.

The indifferent doer
Whose heart is not in his deed,
Stupid and stubborn,
A cheat, and malicious,
The idle lover of delay,
Easily dejected:
He is a man of tamas.

There are three kinds of conscience and three kinds of determination, according to the predominance of each guna. Now listen I will explain them fully, one by one.

A man's conscience has the nature of sattwa, when it can distinguish between the paths of renunciation and worldly desire. Then it knows what actions are right and what are wrong, what is safe and what is dangerous, what binds the embodied spirit and what sets it free. But when the conscience cannot distinguish truly between right and wrong, or know what should and what should not be done, then it has the nature of rajas. And when the conscience is so thickly wrapped in ignorance that it mistakes wrong for right and sees everything distorted then it has the nature of tamas.

Determination inspired by sattwa never wavers. It is strengthened by the practice of yoga. A man who has this kind of determination gains absolute control over his mind, vital energy and senses. Rajas, on the other hand, inspires that kind of determination with which a man follows the object of his desire, or seeks wealth, or does a duty, looking for reward and personal advantage. As for the determination inspired by tamas, it is nothing but obstinacy. It makes a man stubbornly refuse to shake off his dullness, fear, grief, low spirits or vanity.

And now, Arjuna, I will tell you about the three kinds of happiness:

Who knows the Atman
Knows that happiness
Born of pure knowledge:
The joy of sattwa,
Deep his delight
After strict self-schooling:
Sour toil at first
But at last what sweetness,
The end of sorrow.

Senses also
Have joy in their marriage
With things of the senses,
Sweet at first
But at last how bitter:
Steeped in rajas.
That pleasure is poison.

Bred of tamas
Is brutish contentment
In stupor and sloth
And obstinate error :
Its end, its beginning
Alike are delusion.

There is no creature, either on earth or among the devas in heaven, who is free from these three gunas which come forth from Prakriti.

Seer and leader,
Provider and server[1]
Each has the duty
Ordained by his nature
Born of the gunas.

The seer's duty.
Ordained by his nature,

1. See note on Chapter IX, page 150.

Is to be tranquil
In mind and in spirit.
Self-controlled,
Austere and stainless,
Upright, forbearing;

To follow wisdom,
To know the Atman,
Firm of faith
In the truth that is Brahman.

The leader's duty.
Ordained by his nature,
Is to be bold,
Unflinching and fearless,
Subtle of skill
And open-handed,
Great-hearted in battle,
A resolute ruler.

Others are born
To the tasks of providing:

These are the traders,
The cultivators,
The breeders of cattle.

To work for al! men,
Such is the duty
Ordained for the servers,
This is their nature.

All mankind
Is born for perfection
And each shall attain it,
Will he but follow
His nature's duty.

Now you shall hear how a man may become perfect, if he devotes himself to the work which is natural to him. A man will reach perfection if he does his duty as an act of worship to the Lord, who is the source of the universe, prompting all action, everywhere present.

A man's own natural duty, even if it seems imperfectly done, is better than work not naturally his own, even if this is well performed. When a man acts according to the law of his nature, he cannot be sinning. Therefore, no one should give up his natural work, even though he does it imperfectly. For all action is involved in imperfection, like fire in smoke.

When a man has achieved non-attachment, self-mastery and freedom from desire through renunciation, he reaches union with Brahman, who is byond all action.

Learn from me now,
O son of Kunti,
How man made perfect
Is one with Brahman,
The goal of wisdom.

When the mind and the heart
Are freed from delusion,
United with Brahman,
When steady will
Has subdued the senses.
When sight and taste

And sound are abandoned
Without regretting,
Without aversion;
When man seeks solitude,
Eats but little,
Curbing his speech,
His mind and his body.
Ever engaged

In his meditation
On Brahman the truth,
And full of compassion;
When he casts from him
Vanity, violence,
Pride, lust, anger
And all his possessions,
Totally free
From the sense of ego
And tranquil of heart:
That man is ready
For oneness with Brahman.
And he who dwells
United with Brahman,
Calm in mind,
Not grieving, not craving.
Regarding all men
With equal acceptance:
He loves me most dearly.

To love is to know me,
My innermost nature,
The truth that I am:
Through this knowledge he enters
At once to my Being.

All that he does
Is offered before me
In utter surrender: ..
My grace is upon him,
He finds the eternal.
The place unchanging.

Mentally resign all your action to me. Regard me as your dearest loved one. Know me to be your only refuge. Be united always in heart and consciousness with me.

United with me, you shall overcome all difficulties by my grace.

But if your heart is full of conceit, and you do not heed me, you are lost. If, in your vanity, you say "I will not fight," your resolve is vain. Your own nature will drive you to the act. For you yourself have created the karma that binds you. You are helpless in its power. And you will do that very thing which your ignorance seeks to avoid.

The Lord lives in the heart of every creature. He turns them round and round upon the wheel of his Maya. Take refuge utterly in Him. By His grace you will find supreme peace, and the state which is beyond all change.

Now I have taught you that wisdom which is the secret of secrets. Ponder it carefully. Then act as you think best. These are the last words that I shall say to you, the deepest of all truths. I speak for your own good. You are the friend I chose and love.

Give me your whole heart,
Love and adore me.
Worship me always.
Bow to me only.
And you shall find me:
This is my promise
Who love you dearly.
Lay down all duties
In me, your refuge.
Fear no longer,
For I will save you
From sin and from bondage.

You must never tell this holy truth to anyone who lacks self-control and devotion, or who despises his teacher and mocks at Me. But the man who loves Me, and teaches My devotees this supreme truth of the Gita, will certainly come to Me. No one can do Me a higher service than this. No one on earth can be dearer to Me.

And if any man meditates upon this sacred discourse of ours, I shall consider that he has worshipped Me in spirit. Even if a man simply listens to these words with faith, and does not doubt them, he will be freed from his sins and reach the heaven of the righteous.

Have you listened carefully, Arjuna, to everything I have told you? Have I dispelled the delusions of your ignorance?

Arjuna: By Your grace, O Lord, my delusions have been dispelled. My mind stands firm. Its doubts are ended. I will do Your bidding.

Sanjaya:

Such were the words that thrilled my
heart, that marvellous discourse,
Heard from the lips of the high-souled
Prince and the great Lord Krishna
Not with these earthly ears, but by
mystic grace of Vyasa.
Thus I learned that yoga supreme
from the Master of yogis.

Ever and ever again I rejoice, O King,
and remember
Sacred and wonderful truths that
Krishna told to his comrade.
Ever again, O King. I am glad and
remember rejoicing
That most splendid of forms put on
by Krishna, the Sweet One.
Where Lord Krishna is, and Arjuna,
great among archers,
There, I know, is goodness, and peace,
and triumph, and glory.

OM. PEACE. PEACE. PEACE.

APPENDIX

The Cosmology of The Gita

LIKE all other works of Hindu religious literature, the Gita is based upon a clearly-defined system of cosmology. The single, central fact of this cosmology is called Brahman, the Reality. Brahman is the total Godhead. It can never be defined or expressed. The Upanishads say that Brahman is Existence, Knowledge and Bliss; but these are not attributes. Brahman cannot be said to exist. Brahman is Existence itself. Brahman is not wise or happy, but absolute Knowledge, absolute Joy. Another method of approach, more acceptable perhaps to our human minds, is to say: "Brahman is not this, Brahman is not that..", until the entire phenomenal universe has been eliminated, and Brahman alone remains.

Being absolutely present, Brahman is within all creatures and objects. The Godhead is present in man, in the mouse, in the stone, in the flash of lightning. Thus considered, Brahman is called the Atman—a term of convenience merely, which does not imply the slightest difference. The Atman and Brahman are one.

Again, when Brahman is considered in relation to this universe, He is regarded as a personal God, Ishwara. Ishwara is God with attributes. He contains all the divine qualities of love, mercy, purity, justice, knowledge and truth.

Brahman, being the Absolute, is beyond all action. Therefore, Brahman cannot be said to create or to destroy. It is Ishwara, Brahman united with His power who creates this universe, preserves it and dissolves it. To say this is not necessarily to imply a dualism. Brahman's power can no more be separated from Brahman than the heat of fire can be separated from fire itself. But philosophical analysis cannot take us any further into this tremendous mystery. The conception of Ishwara represents all that the human intellect can know of God. Brahman, in the absolute sense, cannot possibly be known by the conscious mind. Brahman can only be experienced in that superconscious state achieved by the saints, which is called samadhi or union with God. The methods of reaching this state are described at length in the Bhagavad Gita. When all sense-contact with the outer world has been broken, by means of discrimination, spiritual discipline and meditation, the mind is able to turn inward upon itself and realize the presence of the Atman, the immanent Godhead. This is the technique of all mystical practice, and it has been taught by every true religion.

Hinduism has further personified the three functions or aspects of Ishwara as Brahma, Vishnu and Shiva. Brahma represents the divine function of creation. Vishnu preservation, and Shiva dissolution. Shiva is often spoken of as "the destroyer," but this is a misleading word, because the universe is never destroyed. Since it is subject to the eternal power of Brahman, the universe is part of a beginningless and endless process, which alternates between the two phases of potentiality and expression. When, at the end of a time-cycle, or kalpa, the universe is dissolved, it passes into a phase of potentiality, a seed-state, and thus awaits its next creation. In Chapter VII of the Gita, this process is described. The phase of expression is called by Sri Krishna, "the day of Brahma," and the phase of potentiality "the night of Brahma." The creatures inhabiting the worlds subject to these cycles are perpetually being reborn and re-dissolved, with each succeeding cosmic day and night. This dissolution should not, however, be thought of as "going back to God." The creature merely returns to the power of Brahman which sent it forth, and remains there in an unmanifested state until the time comes for its re-manifestation.

The power of Brahman is the basis of all mind and matter. It is called Prakriti, or Maya: the terms are interchangeable. According to the Gita, Ishwara makes Himself a body out of Prakriti whenever He chooses to be born among men. Nevertheless, because He is God, He remains master of Prakriti even in His human form. It is in this that the divine incarntion differs from the ordinary mortal. Man, also, is the Atman associated with Prakriti, or Maya. But man is subject to Prakriti, and deluded by It into thinking that he is not the Atman. To become united with the Atman is to throw off this delusion, and to win liberation from the process of birth and death. The liberated man cannot be reborn, because he is no longer subject to the power of Prakriti. The divine incarnation is never subject to this power: he enters the universe and leaves it at will.

Hinduism accepts the belief in many divine incarntions, including

Krishna, Buddha and Jesus, and foresees that there will be many more:

> *"In every age I come back*
> *To deliver the holy,*
> *To destroy the sin of the sinner,*
> *To establish righteousness."*

Prakriti is said to be composed of three forces, known as the gunas. They are sattwa, rajas and tamas. During the "night of Brahma," the phase of potentiality, these gunas are in a state of perfect equilibrium, and Parkriti remains undifferentiated. Creation is the disturbance of this equilibrium. The gunas then begin to enter into a vast variety of combinations, corresponding to the various forms of differentiated mind and matter. Their characteristic may be known from their products in the psychic and physical worlds.

In the physical world, sattwa embodies all that is pure and fine, rajas embodies the active principle, and tamas the principle of solidity and resistance. All three are present in everything, but one guna always predominates. For example, sattwa predominates in sunlight, rajas in an erupting volcano, and tamas in a block of granite.

The gunas also represent the different stages in the evolution of any particular entity. Sattwa is the essence of the form to be realized; tamas is the inherent obstacle to its realization; and rajas is the power by which that obstacle is removed and the essential form becomes manifest.

In the mind of man, sattwa expresses itself psychologically as tranquillity, purity and calmness; rajas as passion, restlessness, aggressive activity; tamas as stupidity, laziness, inertia. Sometimes one guna is predominant, sometimes another; and a man's mood and character vary accordingly. But man can cultivate any one of the gunas, by his actions and thoughts and way of living. We are taught that tamas can be overcome by the cultivation of rajas, and rajas by the cultivation of sattwa. However, the ultimate ideal is to transcend sattwa also and reach the Atman, which is above and beyond the gunas.

In tracing the evolution of differentiated matter from Prakriti. we begin with mahat, the basis of the individual-intelligence. Next comes buddhi, the faculty by which objects are distinguished and classified. Then ahamkara, the ego-sense. Ahamkara divides itself into three functions: (1) manas, which receives impressions from the senses and carries them to buddhi; (2) the five organs of perception—sight, smell, hearing, taste and touch—and the five organs of action—tongue, feet, hands and the organs of evacuation and reproduction—and (3) the five tanmatras, the essences of sound touch, aspect, taste and smell. These subtle tanmatras, combining and recombining, produce the five gross elements, earth, water, fire, air and ether, of which the external universe is composed.

The whole system may be shown diagrammatically, thus:

PRAKRITI

Mahat

Buddhi

Ahamkara

Five Organs of Perception

Five Organs of Action

Manas

Five Tanmatras

Five Gross Elements

We must beware of trying to force the hypotheses of modern western

Science into the frame of the Hindu world picture. Yet certain points of agreement exist between them, and should not be disregarded.

Modern Science has, of course, no concern with the concept of Absolute Reality. It does not seek to know Brahman. Nor does it offer confirmation of the validity of the mystic's claim to superconsciousness. It says, in effect: "For the present, at any rate, we have no technique for investigating this type of experience. When you speak of knowing Brahman you are speaking in extra-scientific terms."

Nevertheless, if we consider Prakriti and the gunas, we find that Science and Vedanta are talking the same language. Science, also, postulates a monistic universe. All matter is made up of different combinations of the chemical elements: and these elements are composed of combinations of identical units. Man is all of a piece with this world and with the most distant of the stars.

Science makes no basic distinction between mind and matter. Mind is everywhere potential. If the scientist cannot yet detect mind in a stone, he believes that this is only because he lacks a suitable method of doing so. He finds no point in evolution at which life can be said to enter, no point at which personality suddenly invests the foetus or the growing infant. Evolution, he tells us, is perfectly continuous, and it has a general direction.

Man's ideals and values are relative, perpetually evolving. The goal is not known, but its direction is apparent, and it is Man's evolutionary mission to move continually toward it, as Columbus sailed toward the unknown West. From the scientific point of view Man's mission is to acquire greater and greater knowledge of his relation to his environment and to gain increasing control over it, since it is really part of himself. And so Arjuna and the scientist are both asking the same question: "What am I?"